Dec. 2005 To Frank
with   Irene

Sou_

An Odyssey into the Feminine

601 (47) £2.00 Du

Elizabeth M Jones

Spiderloom Books

Published by Spiderloom Books
11 Meadow Street, Cardiff, CF11 9PY, UK
www.soul-song.co.uk

British Library Cataloguing in Publication Data.

A CIP catalogue record for this book is available from the British Library

ISBN 978-0-9558626-0-1

Typeset in Palatino by Richard Bryan
Cover Artwork by Kay Leverton
Cover Design by Dek Leverton

Printed by CPI Antony Rowe Ltd.,
Bumpers Farm, Chippenham, England

In loving memory of

Joan and Gordon Jones
and
Susan Mary Bryan

CONTENTS

ACKNOWLEDGEMENTS

So many people have helped and continue to help me on my journey. My huge thanks go to all these generous souls for their inspiration.

With infinite patience, Jan Angelo showed me how to weave my way into my dark corners and how to celebrate all that I found there. Jack Angelo caught me and set me on the path of light.

Myra Fogerty told me that you are never too old to start singing and introduced my to its intricacies. Gilles Petit and John Mount pushed and encouraged me to find my ancestral voice through song and singing.

Angela Morgan Cutler helped me to conceive the shape of this book. Under Susan Richardson's guidance, I honed my writing skills. She read my manuscript, offered her editorial skills and helped me towards the final version of *Soul Song*.

My way to Sound Healing was opened by Jonathan Goldman and his team, particularly the late Saruah, Sarah Benson.

To all my Companions on the Counselling Courses, the Red Road, the Singing Road, the Healing Sound Intensives, the Women of the Red Moon Gatherings and the Writing Group – you all know who you are. Thank you.

Kay Leverton created the sparkling artwork for the cover and for my publishing company's logo and Dek Leverton designed the cover. My thanks for their patience. I am also grateful to Kay for permission to quote from her poetry.

My nephew, Rich Bryan, typeset *Soul Song* and Jules Bryan, and their son in the womb, proofread it. Bless all three of you.

FOREWORD

For many women, finding a voice is an important aspect of self healing and transformation. Those familiar with the writings of journeying woman will acknowledge that this quest is never undertaken lightly. With *Soul Song*, her first published work, Elizabeth invites us to witness her personal quest to find the voice of her authentic Self – uncluttered, undamaged and unlimited by family, relationships, religion, culture, illness and life events. Yet, all these factors take turns in providing us with clues to the existence and loss of this woman's voice. The journey is intense and deep leading to the profound question – did I ever have my own voice? Further Elizabeth ponders: if my voice didn't exist, what does that say about me? Did I exist – where was I amid the rituals of life and living, of growing up, becoming a woman, falling in love, developing a career and so on? Have I ever existed and what about now – who am I? At times, the exploration is light hearted – funny even. But the struggle to get there is heroic – the stuff of mythic proportion. In the depths of despair, grief and emotional pain there is always a healing although, it must be said, not always immediate or evident. But where does this healing come from? Could it be the voice itself urging Elizabeth not to abandon the task but to continue the journey despite apparent dead ends, setbacks, anxieties and real fear? Far from being an intellectual exercise, *Soul Song* sees Elizabeth bring every aspect of her being to the task – her physical, emotional, mental and spiritual self. Further she engages them as "travel consultants" at significant points on the journey. Physical journeying across continents is mirrored by the exploration of inner landscapes, many of which defy explanation other than in sound or song. A new language is required. A new sound is waiting to be birthed. And what of love? Is it the writer's relationship with this elusive, undefinable phenomenon which slumbers at the heart of the search? Could it be that ultimately it is this relationship which determines the outcome of her quest and the birthing of her voice?

Soul Song is an important book for women of all ages and at all stages of awakening. It merits a place on the bookshelf of those interested in, and concerned about, the healing of woman. It has relevance for all those who have accepted the special responsibility of raising the female child.

Read, stay present to yourself, be real and remain open to the messages you give yourself as you bear witness to this woman's journey.

In admiration and gratitude

Jan Angelo

Psychotherapist and Healer

January 2008

Introduction

This book reveals the journey to find my spirituality. The quest began about fifteen years ago and continues to this day. When I began, I didn't understand the nature of what I was looking for, but I was given clues, with help to solve them, along the way. Recovering the sacred feminine and healing the wounded feminine, piece by piece, has been the focus of my task. The process has led me into healing the wounded masculine and integrating the sacred masculine. For it is through the marriage of these two energies, the feminine and the masculine, that spirituality is to be found.

The idea for writing the book came to me, one evening, several years ago. I was lying in the bath musing about self-help books.

They're helpful, yes. All sorts of advice about how to… meditate, how to… find your spirituality, how to…deal with your anger, how to…feel your fear, how to …cope with your depression, how to …find the feminine. But they irritate me as well. Few, if any, of them seem to talk about how painful it can be to follow their advice. Often I find I am stopped in my tracks on my own journey and I don't know why. Maybe another book can help me. But it can't. So my thirst for more of "This Way" books can never be assuaged. What I would like to read is a book by somebody who has done some of these things and tells of what happened to them in the doing.

1

What did they experience? Was it frightening, did they rage, cry, hurt? Did they have all the sorts of horrible feelings I was having? Did they want to give up? How did they keep going? The fear and pain of clearing through old wounds rarely seems to be mentioned. Well, why don't I write about what I'm doing? Write the sort of book I'd find helpful. And maybe someone else on their journey might find it useful. It might even inspire them. Writing it might inspire me.

And so the idea of a book was born. It will be the story of an odyssey to find the truth of myself. The terrain will be that of an explorer who scales rugged mountains to place flags on high peaks, and sometimes falls off. Who sails the seas' wild waves, rides river rapids and is swept under the waters to find calm oceans. Who crosses arid deserts looking for life-saving oases. Who enters raging volcanoes to find the source of the fire. Who encounters the bitter east winds and flies on the thermals of the balmy southern breezes. Who enters the dark caves of the West to dream her dream. Who freezes in the North to commune with the spirits of the ancestors. It will be a quest inward to my interior world and outward to the exterior world.

Where should I start? With my journal, of course. I began keeping it during a time of therapy and, to date, it covers a period of about twenty years. It has become the place where I take the events of my exterior world to the interior, to watch and hear them as they unfold undreamed of significance. It's where I re-write the story of my life into something which fits me. But how could I take miles of writing and bring some kind of order to apparent chaos? I wanted to be faithful to the unfolding journey even though I often didn't understand at the time the connections between events and changes in my thinking and the way I was living my life. But as I re-read the journals, with the benefit of hindsight I began to decipher the connecting threads. And so *Soul Song*, which covers a period of eight years of my journey, is constructed around experiences of the events of my inner and outer life. Courses, workshops, therapy, singing, travelling, writing, dreaming, imagining, thinking, conversations, ceremony and ritual all feed, in me, upon each other.

If you have picked up this book I hope it might inspire you on your journey.

Chapter One

Crushed Velvet

Chapter One

Crushed Velvet

'Come quickly, your mother's condition has worsened.'

'Has she…?'

'You need to come. Now.'

I put the telephone down, transfer my calls and dash from the office. Speeding along streets filled with rush hour traffic I think of the many times I've made similar journeys from work to hospital, wondering if my mother will be alive when I get there. They are too many to count. Always she has been, surviving to continue her physically frail journey for yet more years.

'I'm past my sell-by date,' she says often. 'I've been kept alive for long enough by operations and pills and potions.'

And I say, 'You come from tough Irish peasant stock.'

In spite of this avowed wish to depart, letting go of her physical life has been hard for her to do; it has not come to her quickly or easily. Throughout these last five weeks, since she had a stroke, I have watched her struggle with the choice of whether or not to leave now. What lessons is she learning? She cannot eat or drink and her movement and speech have all but departed. But a decision is still to be made. Night descends in the thirty minutes it takes me to get to the hospital. Along the country road leading to it, an ambulance speeds by in the opposite direction, its blue light flashing silently in the wet darkness. In the car park, I leap out over the tarmac to the former sanatorium. Inside, the corridor stretches without end towards the ward. At its door the Sister, her mouth moving, her hands waving like a mime artist, waits for me.

'You've just missed your mother. She's been taken back to the acute hospital. Go quickly.'

Ah, the ambulance.

'Is she alive?'

The Sister shrugs her shoulders.

Maybe, maybe not. Why have they moved her, I want to ask? But it is a pointless question; it will waste time I might no longer have. I run to my car, to return part of the way I have come, following the route taken by the speeding, swaying light.

At the next hospital I sit in a room labelled "Emergency Admissions Waiting Room" and wait. It is empty of any other humans, but I seek a dim quiet corner in which to hide. There is none. Harsh white light finds every corner of the room. This is a place of no privacy, with nowhere to hide from the truth. I feed a machine with some money and it delivers a cup of hot black coffee. That is what the label says, but the taste of the first single scalding sip tells me it might be tea or even soup. I do not want the drink, but it has been something to do. Now its usefulness is over.

Seats line the walls; one of them waits for me. *Shall I sit?* I lower myself and, as I touch the cracked vinyl-covered stuffing, a magnet pulls me upward.

I stand.

My feet move off, drawn by my eyes to a poster on the wall. I have seen it now, but I don't know what's in it.

There's a picture over there, something else to look at. Palm trees bend in the wind towards the … *I'll just wander around.* I'm not disturbing anybody except myself.

So much thought about such small decisions, which once made no longer seem right.

A nurse announces, 'The doctor will see you now.'

How deeply absorbed I have been by my dilemma, not to wonder or worry about what is happening to my mother, for it is happening without any help from me. In a cubby-hole of a room filled with a desk bare of anything, I slide into a chair facing the doctor, a young woman with ancient eyes.

'In cases like this…'

My mother is a case, I realise.

'…. we would recommend a heart pacemaker…'

'Oh no,' I cry. 'Surely not with her history. Not how she's been the last five weeks and…'

Could this doctor imagine doing such a thing? Fifteen years ago, a surgeon told me early one Christmas morning after emergency surgery that my mother's heart was perishing. She might live for just a year or two more. He did not know my mother! But she has been readying herself over these past few weeks to leave. How cruel to make her stay.

The doctor continues. 'But, in her case, we wouldn't recommend it.'

At last, it's time for the medical profession to rest its wares. I do not want to ask the next question, but my tongue takes over.

'How long will it be do you think?' Although my mind is filled with thoughts of her impending death, as I reach the need to use the word, I cannot say it. But "it" is enough. The doctor knows what I mean. She has been waiting for me to ask the question for without it she will not volunteer the information.

'Not long.'

'May I see her?'

In another room my mother lies on a trolley. Her eyes are shut and an oxygen mask helps her breath. Her grey hair is silver under the bright lights. She seems relaxed. I take her hand. I dare to for she is not conscious. Awake, she might ask sharply, 'What are you doing?' And I, the accused child would be left wondering what's wrong. I hear myself say, *I want to.* She says, *Don't be silly.* That has been her way, so it has been mine.

One nurse passes on information to another for her notes, 'In the ambulance so many milligrams of... were administered.'

So, her heart stopped in the ambulance. They brought her back. My head buzzes. Why prolong her life when she wants to go? A porter arrives to take us up to the ward. We're a small procession. I carry her few possessions from the last hospital placed in a large plastic bag. He steers my mother on the trolley, with practised ease, along corridors filled with strolling visitors and takes us into a lift.

'Just caught me before I go to tea,' he says cheerfully. 'Been here before?'

'Yes, many times.'

'Your Mum?'

'Yes, she is.'

'We'll soon have her comfy.'

We arrive at the room where my mother is to have the privacy of spending her last hours.

'Cheerio love. All the best.' The porter disappears.

And now I sit beside her bed. The nurses have settled her but she hasn't been disturbed by all the activity. On the other side of the door, I hear the staff going about their business. Conferring, sharing their personal ups and downs in their spare moments throughout the night. Through the large uncurtained window the inkiness of night locks us into this small white room, one bed, one locker, one armchair. I cling to the edge of the chair, wondering what I should be doing. I am afraid. My mother is dying and I don't know how to be. Is there anything I must do? For so many years I've lived with this half-recognised, unreasonable and self-imposed task of thinking somehow or other that being there for my mother comes before everything else. I have been unable to break the habit. I don't want to sit here steeped in worry. I want to sit here in love. *This is a vigil* I hear a voice saying. I look around but see no one. But someone is with us. Yes, that's right; this is a vigil. I'm waiting, watching, witnessing. I can sit here full of fear, worrying, wondering what is going to happen. Or, I can wait and honour the passing of this life of the woman who bore me into this world, who tutored me in its ways for better or for worse. My mother, the one person who has known me for longer than any other and whom I have known for longer than any other. I lean back in my chair into the shadows and pick up a lavender bag, a gift from a thoughtful friend. I sniff it and the muscles holding my body in tense anticipation relax. My mind drops its guard and sieves through the events of the five weeks since my mother's stroke and drifts back to….

Another bed, another ward in this same hospital, three weeks ago. It is evening and I have come from work to see my mother. She lies propped on pillows, her eyes shut, her mouth lopsided. I have spoken to her, but she doesn't seem to be aware of me. Perhaps she will wake up.

The lady in the next bed leans over. 'She was awake earlier. Your mother?'

'Yes. Has she said anything?'

'Just mumbles something if I speak to her. Lovely smile, hasn't she.'

I wait with Mum for half an hour and then an hour. I'm just being with her, my feet resting on the end of her bed. Unlike many other visits she has no questions, no avid requests for news of my and others' doings and comings and goings. No demands to 'get me out of here.' She's about her own business. It is time for me to leave. I bend over and kiss her goodbye.

As she half opens her eyes she mumbles, 'I love you.'

I am startled. I don't ever remember her saying those words to me. Such a long wait for what I have longed to hear.

As tears roll down my face I say, 'I love you too, Mum.'

Her brown eyes smile and then close. Have I ever said those words to her? Do they make a difference? I don't know. My sadness tells me of finding something I have missed for so long.

Another visit. It's eight o'clock in the morning, before I go to work, and I've popped in to see her after talking to the doctors. They want to insert a feeding tube and I've signed the papers. There's a brightness and eagerness in her face that is faded by the time I usually see her in the evenings.

She mumbles, 'Where's Dad?'

'I don't know.' I'm startled. He has been dead for nine years.

'He's been here and now he's gone.' This, I am sure, is what she has mumbled.

She is confused, I think. But no, it is as though he has been with her and I have just missed him. As an afterthought I wonder if she's talking about her father. He died more than thirty-five years ago. I wonder if Narna, who helped to look after her when she was very young, is there too? Mum once told me that she was the person who she hoped would be waiting for her when she crossed over. I have a sense of family and friends who have passed over gathering to help her make this journey.

Yet another visit just a few days ago, as pneumonia settles into her body. I sit at her bedside. The nurses have pinned her "Get Well" cards to the wall alongside her bed. There is no response from her though I tell her what has been happening. I ask if she would like me to put some oil on her hands. Silently, without opening her eyes, she brings her left hand from under the sheet and I massage lavender and geranium oils across her palms and around her fingers. The scents of green citrus and earthy lavender hit me in the middle of my brow and sink into her skin to do their work. As I finish, her right hand appears.

Now, as I look at my mother, her face and upper body lie in a pool shining from a golden globe above her bed. Sparks of dust flitter in the light and disappear into darkness beyond. She tugs the oxygen mask away from her face.

I put it back whispering, 'It helps you to breath, Mum.'

Her hands and arms, these of this eighty-two-year-old grandmother, become those of a young woman as they draw graceful languid curves, caressing the air about her. Their shadow images scroll across the white walls of the room. Their movement is unceasing, and purposeful as a spider weaving a web. Do I know this woman?

Do you remember the ottoman filled with old clothes for dressing up, I hear myself asking myself. *Yes, here it is. I lift the lid, its fabric worn thin by years of wear from children's expectant hands. Lying within, tumbled heaps of silks and satins, suits and skirts, pale pink and vivid violet, drab beige and dark khaki. I rummage through layers. Here's a hat belonging to my aunt, my mother's glamorous eldest sister. It's rose-coloured with a huge floppy brim. Before my day, my sister floated it in a bath of water. My mother told the story of the hours she spent drying it out and re-shaping it in the hope her sister wouldn't come to know its fate. Ah, here's what I'm looking for. Heaps of crushed ivory, unironed in years, slip by my head, to skim my body and hug my knees. They fall in folds around my feet. This wedding velvet is scented with exotic lily faded by time. The shoes, satin and narrow have heels so high, I teeter on toes crowded to a point. I trip through a river of ivory train, tattered and yellowed. Pouting and preening, with lips reddened by my sweeties, I twirl and process as my mother might have done. What were her dreams when she wore this dress? Did she live them or lose them, forget them or put them aside? Or did they just fade away?*

Until now I have never been able to connect the mother I know with the woman who wore this dress, the woman who now lies upon this starch-layered bed, her breath uneven in and weighty out. I think of her as a stoic. So ill, so often, for so long. How many times has she faced the immediacy of death? I can't count.

It's been rare for her to speak to me of her feelings about anything or anybody in her life. In later years when she does talk, the occasions are all the more powerful for their rarity. During another time, in another hospital, she tells me about one event of her life.

'War had been declared on Germany. Dad's job and my Dad's building business had disappeared almost overnight. There I was on a train returning from London to Cardiff.'

Her eyes glaze over. I try to imagine her gazing through steam-encrusted windows, watching fields and towns speed past. Mum must have been about twenty-five, Annie, my eldest sister, about four.

'You must have been six or seven months pregnant with Sue.'

'Yes. And you hadn't even been thought of. Dad had gone on ahead and had found a job in Cardiff.' Her eyes filled with tears. 'Everything had gone; home, Dad's job, money.'

This is a side of my mother I've never seen before.

'And I was going to have to live with my mother in law. She thought I wasn't good enough to be her son's wife. I knew she was going to be pretty nasty to me. It was the worst time of my life.'

That's all she would say. In all the years of my parents' reminiscences about the war, not once did they speak of terror, despair or even boredom. Tales of events and exploits were told as though an episode from *Dad's Army*, designed to entertain with laughter. I guess that's all they could bear to remember. My mother says she knitted Fair Isle sweaters and smocked young girls' dresses through the long, lonely evenings when we were in bed; her husband patrolling the roofs of his office lest incendiary bombs fall from the sky and fires have to be put out. How much has she kept hidden from others and how much from herself? In these last years of hers it's as though all the secret fears of her life have broken through. None of them seem to be for herself but for her children and grandchildren. I remember a week I spent in West Wales with friends. I sent her a postcard describing a walk along the cliff tops, then sitting, watching seals swimming in waters off the coast. The morning she received it, she telephoned where I was staying.

'Are you all right?' Her words were clipped.

'Yes. Didn't you get my postcard?'

'That's what I'm ringing about. How dare you put yourself in such danger. You could have fallen over the cliffs.'

I had been telling her that I was well, happy and enjoying myself.

As I watch her unawareness now, her eyelids lift and I lean forward.

'Hello Mum.'

She smiles and moves her lips. But what she says, I don't

know. Her speech is muffled by the paralysis, which has over-taken her body.

'Your hair's getting very long and it's silky straight. You'll be able to put it up soon.' As long as I can remember she's always had short hair and a perm.

She seems to understand my words and laughs silently but joyfully and bodily as a child. Her eyes, which have been filmed and dulled, sparkle and speak of what once was mysterious, but now is known to her, though not to me.

She once asked me, 'Are you afraid of dying?'

'Yes, I am. But I'm not sure why. Are you?'

'No. But I'm afraid of what comes afterwards?'

'Do you mean there might be nothing?"

'No. But how will I know the afterwards?'

At the time I puzzled over her answer and still do. What does it mean? Is there a way of knowing, of sensing the essence of everything without any of the clues we use in ordinary, everyday life? Now my mother is discovering that place and knows it. Everything in this moment feels all right. I don't have to worry about her any longer. Her eyelids close and I see the years retreating across her face. The toil of fear, worry, anger, sorrow, disappointment no longer clutter her way. For now, I don't want to feel the sadness of her leaving, for I might miss witnessing her departure. But I do feel I'm losing a mother who has been a secret, which she has kept from me. And now I am allowed just a glimpse. Everything is changing in a way that for the moment I can only sense.

Twenty-four hours later my mother dies. One last breath and I see her fly off to join the cawing gulls circling on the other side of the window in the brilliant sun of the early spring morning. For one moment I am envious of the return her spirit is making to its home. Had she not delayed her departure for these two days, I would not know that death could be something to be embraced rather than feared. But I am resentful too. She has gone. And I am left with the enigma I still have to solve.

Who am I? What am I?

Chapter Two

Wheels of Light

Chapter Two

Wheels of Light

I return to a time several years before my mother died.

I didn't know it then, but I was beginning to stumble from one life to another. I had discovered a lump in my breast. I saw my doctor who referred me to the hospital's breast clinic with the instruction that if I hadn't received an appointment within a week I was to let her know. She wouldn't tell me if she thought it was cancer, but I was pretty sure it must be. My mother had had it fifteen years earlier. I returned home that evening, sat down and started to cry. How was I going to cope with the uncertain days to come? Within a few minutes, energy, so powerful, rose through my body and I had to get up and race around the house shouting. After about half an hour I came to a stop. I sat down again and knew, somehow or other, that I would manage. It was cancer, and a few weeks later I had a mastectomy. My physical recovery was quick. But over the following months I began to question how I was living my life. Rage spluttered out of me, ejecting me from what I had thought was a safe cocoon of work, family and friends into a world in which I had no idea where, or even whether there was a place in it for me. What was I doing? Where was I going? I felt so out of step with everyone around me.

One lunchtime, as I was leaving the public library, quite by chance I saw a leaflet for a stress and relaxation weekend at the local college of music and drama. Maybe I could at least learn how to relax. It was there that an aromatherapist taught us how to massage our hands and feet with essential oils such as lavender, rosemary and geranium added to a base oil. She also gave each of us a voucher for a half-price treatment. Though it took me several months, in great trepidation, I made an appointment and so began my excursion into another world.

The magical properties of healing oils and gentle massage and the spirit guides of the therapist started to awaken me. What is this thing called spirituality? Do I have it; can I get it? I didn't know what the word meant or why I was asking. I read a few books but I couldn't grasp what 'it' was in relation to me. The aromatherapist gave me details of two series of workshops facilitated by Jack Angelo, which she said could help me find some answers to my questions.

And so I joined a group and started to learn about healing, the channelling of energy from its source to someone in need of help. Here I discovered that we have many more bodies than just the physical, the energy of each vibrating at successively higher speeds than light. The etheric body can be seen as a misty material, or felt by the hands, projecting just a couple of inches beyond the physical body. It contains a complete blueprint of the physical body. Next, the astral or emotional body is the one we all enter when we sleep. Emotions such as fear live at its lower levels; at its higher levels we find unconditional love. The mental body processes energies like creative and intuitive thought. The spiritual or soul body is where all experiences are gathered and are a record of a soul's experience. Information about all these levels is available to us through our ability to sense and perceive energy in forms subtler than just the physical. The combined effect of all these bodies produces a multi-coloured aura of light around the physical body, which can be felt even if not seen.

Then I enrolled for a series of seven workshops, lasting over a period of four months, to make a healing journey through the seven major energy centres. Known as chakras, these wheels of spinning energy are gateways, aligned with the spine of the body, into the etheric level. I learned about the parts of the body, the energies and the levels of awareness associated with each energy centre and their links with each other and with our personal development. The chakras carry the energies of what we are and feel, how we think, change, express ourselves and create. They help us gain awareness of ourselves in ways other than thinking about ourselves. They are a totally different way of looking at who we are.

And so I began to discover that I definitely was not who I thought I was.

Whats' in the Light?

My hands and senses, not my thoughts, Jack says, are to be the focus of the work of spiritual healing. It is unlikely my mind will understand much of what goes on. *Quite!*

I've managed to get myself to this dimly lit church hall for a workshop An Introduction to Spiritual Healing. *I could be sick at any moment. I won't allow it.* It's a Saturday in May and there are twenty of us here, sitting in a round on hard upright chairs. I'm here because I am lost to myself. This is my secret lurking behind what I think of as a calm, efficient exterior. My desperate unknowingness of what to do, where to go, how to keep my life spinning away from me has brought me into this circle. The hall is almost a basement, so there's little natural light coming through the windows on one side of the room only. I don't know anybody here. But Jack and his wife Jan have welcomed me. I've only spoken to Jack on the phone until now and he's not a bit as I imagined. He's got a beard. I wasn't expecting that.

We are underway. I rub my hands together as instructed and hold them palms facing each other, body width apart in front of me. I move them closer together and a prickling sensation rises up through their flesh to spread across the skin, as a magnetic pull bounces them back and forth gently. The palms are speckled red, a bit like a rash. These are signs of the energy emanating from my hands.

I learn first how to sense, through my hands, another person's aura. My partner stands in front of me. I shut my eyes to help quieten my thoughts, to concentrate on what I sense. My hands move towards her body and begin to tingle, then they stop. They start again and fill with heat; it disappears almost as soon as I notice it. *I'm not doing this right.* Ah, my hands are very warm again; they're being pushed out farther from the body, around a bump or bulge. Now they're moving closer again. I have completed the scan. *What am I doing here? These are workshops for healers. I'm not one.* A number of people are, and seem to know what they are doing. They talk of experiences they remember having as children, like seeing people's auras as coloured light around their heads. *This is so different from anything I've done before. I could be on another planet.*

With another partner I practise finding the chakras. He sits on a chair; I stand at his side, ready to begin. Holding my hands a few inches from his body I start opposite the bottom of his spine. It is possible to sense the quality of the energy of the chakras as colour, feelings, sounds, thoughts, or all of these. I move my hands while watching the imagined screen in my head. Nothing appears, except a sense of emptiness. In front of the sacral, just below the navel, my hands tingle and instead of orange, the colour when this chakra is in balance, patches of brown and grey appear on my screen. *No sense now in wondering what it means.* In front of the solar plexus chakra, as my hands are halted, I sense a barrier. Over the heart chakra in the centre of my partner's chest, there is nothing. *This is hopeless. I don't know what I'm doing. Never mind just move up to the throat.* Now I hear someone singing in distant hills. At the final two chakras, the brow, in the middle of the forehead, and the crown, on top of the head, my hands start prickling and grow hot. There's a great deal of activity here. *Someone else's thoughts might be busy.* I have finished and my partner and I share our experiences. What I've sensed seems so little, yet he can relate it to what's happening in his life.

With yet another partner I practise healing. I scan her aura but I'm at a loss to know where to start. *Don't direct. Go where you're taken.* My hands are drawn as the heat builds up through my body. It flows as a multitude of silver threads from me into my partner. I stand silently, experiencing the ebb and flow; snaking along channels through me and from me. *But what's going on now? I feel peculiar, shaky; I'm going to faint. I haven't felt like this before. I can see my arms in front of me but I can't feel them connected to the rest of my body.* The heat is dying away and my hands cool. The healing is complete. My partner tells me she could feel lots of heat going to a part of her body where, for a number of years, she's experienced pain. I'm intrigued. Somehow or other my hands knew where the healing energy needed to go. Weeks later my partner tells me that the pain has disappeared and not returned since the healing. *It's nothing to do with me. She's just trying to make me feel good; it must be to do with something else that happened to her.*

Jack introduces us to distant healing. Healing is an energy that can be sent in unseen ways to someone not present, and at a distance physically from the healer. The person may be someone whom I know and seeks healing or someone who appears to me. *I don't understand, but that doesn't mean it can't happen.* We are preparing to practise. It's late afternoon, and the lights in the church hall are lowered. I stand in the dimness, not aware of the other participants around me. I hold my hands out in front of me, affirming my intention of linking my higher self with the Source, even though I don't seem to know either of them. I ask in my head for whoever wishes for healing to come into the light. I wait. Thoughts flit in and out of my head. *How will I know when someone comes? How will I know who it is? What do I have to watch for? What shall I do? Will my sister who died fourteen years ago come or maybe my father - he died six years ago - or maybe my mother, who's not well? Be calm, be patient.* My hands begin to tingle and I feel heat travelling through my body; it feels much stronger than before. A scene, empty of everything, appears in the way that part of a darkened stage-set is illuminated slowly by a spotlight. A faint figure appears, fuzzy at first then growing in definition. It is my uncle, who has been dead for some five years. He stands in front of me in the blue and grey check dressing gown he wore the last time I saw him. He is a vivid figure and though I can't see his face, there's no mistaking his essence. He's not looking at me, not aware of me. I want to touch him. I could put my hand out but I don't. I sense he doesn't know where to go. I stand holding him in the circle of light. Tears begin to roll down my face as I sense he is lost. Slowly the heat in my hands disappears, the light dims and my uncle leaves. I have no idea how long he has been here.

It hasn't entered my mind that this uncle would come. I wonder why he has. I remember the last time I saw him. He was in a hospice; the cancer was tightening its grip. We took a short walk from his bed to look at the sea through the window. He asked if I could make any sense of what life was about. I don't remember his precise words or all he said or, what I said. But I felt he was revealing a hidden part of himself. I didn't have any answers for him or for myself. All I could do was listen. On the other side of the window, waves slapped on the rocks below, as they had done for eternity. Out there, the world had such a sense of continuity while on the inside my uncle was dying with one huge question on his mind; the only question that matters in the end.

After his funeral, my aunt asked if I would like any of his many books. I dipped into the heavy, hardback volumes of philosophical works. Here and there sentences were underlined and seemed to sum up his search for the meaning of his life. He had been seeking answers for a long time.

I am not surprised he has come for healing.

So What's in the Base?

Does a stone have a history?

In spite of myself, the sessions on Spiritual Healing have drawn me into the mystery of who I am. It's the middle of July and I am back in the same church hall with Jack and Jan and twenty-one other people, some of whom I know from the Healing Workshop. Rogue rays of sun have found their way through the tall grimy basement windows to shine across our circle. Specks of dust emerge from their hidden places. They dance in the light, before returning to loiter in unseen recesses. I am here on an inward pilgrimage. Perched on the edge of a wooden seat, I hear the words chakras and auras and know that I only understand them vaguely. I'm sitting next to Bob, who's a carpenter. He twiddles his beard.

'Are you nervous?'

I can barely say, 'Yes.'

'Me too.'

It's a mistake to have come. But I can't possibly leave now we've started. I'm going to have to take a lot on trust and see what sense I can make of it over the months.

We begin at the base chakra. This is where we know and accept who we are on this planet and where we celebrate the need to change. There is talk of setting our own goals, however we describe them. *Goals! A word conjuring up images of hockey matches at school, goals at work. But where am I going? To find myself! I can't be more specific than that.* I am touching the depth and width of my incomprehension. We need to decide our direction, be aware of pitfalls and know that we will be challenging norms constantly. We need weapons, because we will have to fight. *How can I decide my direction when I don't understand what it is I'm looking for? And I am going to have to fight!* My mood flattens and I try to catch what little optimism I have before it dwindles away.

But it's here that I am introduced to my imagination, the language of the soul. Jack asks us to imagine ourselves in our base chakra. When it is in balance it vibrates to the colour red. I find my way to its place at the base of my spine, and send roots deep into the earth through my feet planted on the scored wooden floorboards. I settle all my attention there and wait. Fussy thoughts bustle around. *What's going on here? Why am I doing this? It won't work.* From stillness, established beyond my thinking awareness, a many-petalled bloom of rosy red opens and a little girl rises from its centre. I can't see who she is. *Maybe she's me.* I'm dancing around, jumping from cloud to cloud, spinning in the air. Lots of people pop up from behind clouds demanding to know what I think I am doing. I tell them in a very loud voice to "Push Off". And they do. They've got my message. Good. I'm having a grand time. Alone in a blue and white check dress, I feel the brush of warm breezes against my skin as my body tumbles through the air, arms wide, legs springing, hair bobbing over my eyes. My blue ribbon has fallen out. Then without any instruction from me, I become a graceful young girl in her white tutu, executing a series of complicated ballet steps, so light and delicate, not a dent appears in frothy, white clouds. From inside me pours a song I have never heard before, so powerful and insistent it seems everybody must hear as it explodes from my lungs and rings in my ears. Surely I must be disturbing those around me.

I open my eyes. They are absorbed in their own experiences. *They must be deaf.*

I close my eyes. Oh no! The singer has melted away. Where is she? I shouldn't have opened my eyes. I try to pull her back but each time she begins to appear she is replaced by a powerful figure wearing trousers, striding across my horizon, stealing into my imagination. Its feet sink through greying clouds and stumble into thick, elastic mud collecting on its boots and pulling it down. I can't lift my feet anymore. The exhilaration of floating above the clouds has disappeared. I do not want to stay in this earthen straightjacket. I want to be way above the clouds, singing and dancing. I struggle to free myself but I am locked into a black, oozing bog. I am weighted down from the inside. My stomach trembles, bile rises to my throat. I do not want to know this person who feels powerfully restraining. I have had enough. I'll think about something else. Row upon row of chicken dinners pass across my internal screen. Perhaps I'll have chicken for dinner. I wonder if I'll have enough energy to go out with friends tonight. This is tiring work.

At last it is time to come back from my imagination.

♫

Over the following two weeks before the next workshop, I try to embrace the images of the singing and dancing girl in my spare moments at home. I sway through the rooms of my house to the music of *Swan Lake*, trying to remember the ballet steps of my childhood. I stamp the rhythm of the flamenco. I open my mouth and sing the blues of *Summertime* with the words I think I do not know. At times I feel powerful energy in my body; it lifts me off the ground. I am a huge scarlet balloon. If I cut the string I won't have to stay. I will be free to float away, drifting in the windless blue reaches above the clouds, untouched by other's opinions. I can fly wherever I want. But a force pulls me back to earth with red rage, a now familiar but unwelcome companion. With no outlet, it chains me to the earth with nowhere to go. I do not feel free to use the power of the singing, dancing child. But I have touched it. I want to own it. What stops me? About a week after the workshop, I am at work and, through the window next to my desk, I see university students collecting gowns and mortarboards for their graduation day. That evening, at home, I wonder what compelled me to watch the comings and goings. The day has been sunny just like the day I graduated. Recollections begin to trickle through.

A blazing, August afternoon in an endless summer when the sun has shone each day without break since my finals at Reading University finished at the end of May, sixteen years ago. Underfoot the grass has burned away leaving cracked red earth worn smooth by hundreds of pairs of feet of graduands and their families. I sink further into the now of then. Dust in the heavy air stifles my nostrils. Perspiration pours from my hands. I wipe them yet again on the faded, black gown before going up to shake hands and collect my degree. I do not want to be here. I slip into the flatness of that moment and feel a weight of nothingness. But there is something in it. It is heavy. I cannot lift it. I turn back a corner. I have spent three years gaining an honours degree in psychology. I am not excited. I feel no sense of achievement, just disinterest.

Now, sixteen years later, a tear creeps from the corner of my left eye and trickles a crooked path over my cheek to fall onto the collar of my jacket. I can see it spreading through the material into an irregular patch. Disappointment coagulates then floods through my body and I listen to its weight. I so much want this time to mark a move into a new way of life; but it does not. This, which has lain dormant like a song in a stone until now, grows and burgeons as it pours forth. I cannot stop it. I don't want to. I am in it, tossed and tumbled, gasping for air, drawn back again into the wild waters of a mountainous sea waiting for sixteen years to be noticed, heard, felt.

♫

I write in my journal a few days after recalling these memories. Why have I allowed myself never to feel? It's as though I have been told all my life not to dwell on failure, not to reveal my feelings to myself. *Well*, the rebel says, *I will reveal some of myself.* Is that wise I wonder? *Yes,* says the rebel. I sit by the light of a candle and let my hand write a list of the things my teenager loathes about herself: lank, shapeless hair; spotty face; tall, ungainly body. No matter how hard I try, I always look scruffy. Here's a photograph of me during my first year at grammar school. It's a Christmas present for my grandparents. On the back, in my careful sloping handwriting: 'Hope this doesn't spoil your Christmas.' My mother says when she looks at the photo, 'For goodness sake, why didn't you straighten your collar and tie, and comb your hair?' She doesn't believe me when I say I did. My posture is appalling, my P.E. teacher tells me. I know it is. She doesn't understand how important it is for me to hide myself. I am five feet seven inches tall, twelve years old and tower over all my friends, girls and boys. I feel so plain, so very plain. This is an image of myself, which I carry around inside me, even now. There is nobody who can hear how miserable I am, not even me.

But there must have been some happy times.

Joy and Sorrow

Somewhere inside me I am beginning to sense that my joy and sorrow are somehow muddled up together. It is two weeks since the last workshop and I am back in the dusty church hall with faces that are becoming familiar. There's a sense of nervous excitement about. Outside it's the end of July and Cardiff is basking in a baking day. But it's cool here in the dim basement.

At the end of the last workshop Jack asked each of us to bring to today's meeting something linking orange, joy and creativity, for our exploration of the second chakra, the sacral;

it vibrates to this colour. I've brought an excerpt from *The Prophet* entitled *Joy and Sorrow* and decorated it in orange. As I'm full of the usual unknowingness and apprehension, I vow here and now to give up thinking and worrying about what is going on. If I can stop trying so hard to work things out for just part of the time, maybe something will click, even though I might not be aware of it at the time. This chakra, Jack tells us, is where we experience our sexuality - the balance of masculine and feminine energies in our bodies, and where we find the energies of creativity and joy. It is the place of the "giggle factor". The thought for the day is about learning from natural life, from trees, from rocks.

The magnolia tree in my garden doesn't have to learn anything. But I can learn from it. I like that idea. All it needs to express itself is contained in its seed deep in the earth. As it lies there, watered by the rain, warmed by the rays of the sun, lit by the movements of the moon, it doesn't need constant instruction to grow into its shape, height, or colour. It doesn't have to be told, you're not putting in enough effort; you don't fit in here; don't go there; come here. It offers its gifts of rose-hearted petals and green canopy each year, unasked. When its branches are left bare, it stands firm but flexible through winter's winds awaiting spring; roots spread beneath the earth, secure in their place.

As I sense a huge legacy of experience weighing me down with expectations having nothing to do with me, we are introduced to The Orange Tree of Life and Growth. Jack asks us to describe three things we will do and three feelings we will have, to reach the top of the tree where divine love and wisdom are expressed. *I have absolutely no idea. I can't understand the questions let alone think of any answers.* My thoughts slip from frenetic activity to a blank sheet until, in a visualisation, Jack asks us to sit in an orange flower and wait to be shown where we need to go. *What am I meant to be doing? Do I have to make something happen?* I fidget on my hard chair. *What are other people doing? Are they still here? I'll just check. That person looks like he's having a blissful time. I wish I were.* I remind myself of my vow to rest my mind and, closing my eyes, I relax my body.

I am facing a narrow ravine. It's opened below me while I wasn't looking. I'm hanging by my feet from a tightrope stretched from one side to the other. It is deep and dark; I can't see to the bottom. The sides are steep and rocky as they stretch away into the blackness. *This is a foolhardy way of travelling.* As I think this, I rescue myself from the thin rope and begin to climb down into the ravine. I have no sense of the ground beneath my feet, of any paths or footholds. The descent doesn't take long. I reach a place of rest on a ledge. I don't know whether I've reached the bottom or not but this is as far as I go. I ask for help and wait in the darkness. I don't want to think about where I am or what might lie in the thin air around me. How long I remain here I don't know, but nothing appears. At last, Jack chimes the bell and calls us back to the present. *I'm fed up. Nobody's appeared even when I asked for help and that's not easy to do anyway. But I'm not surprised.* He asks us to talk about

41

what happened during our visualisations. I pluck up courage and describe my experience.

He says, 'The ravine is significant for you, though in what way, you will need to discover.'

Ha, very helpful!

During the tea break, this experience sets me off on a train of thought. Quite why I don't know, but it is an insight into my childhood. *Mum and Dad took great pains to ensure they treated my two sisters and me equally. There was to be no favouritism. I think, as a child I learned I was no different from my sisters. I was a separate physical being. But it feels as though scrupulous fairness has blanked out any feelings I had of being different. Of being an individual in any way other than physically. I have no sense of being separate, unique. I think I'm beginning to touch a profound part of myself that I have been divorced from. For how long? For as long as I can remember.*

At home, some days after the workshop, in my imagination I take myself back into the deep ravine and again ask for help. I relax and wait. An Indian woman emerges into the light. She wears a green silk sari and sits in a gutter, at the side of a dusty road in India. The sun beats down on her mercilessly. I am looking at her as she raises her head and holds her hands out to me as though entreating me to approach. *Who are you? I have come in answer to your request for help. I bring kindness and*

compassion and will help you find your wellspring. She disappears. But there is more I want to ask her, more answers I need. I wish I could make these images stay longer and show me a lot more. For days I wonder about the beautiful sari. Why does she sit in a gutter in India? What does my wellspring mean? But she has come in answer to my request for help. I hope she will come again, for I don't understand what she means. My mood, though, is changed by her visit. I have a sense of excitement, expectation. And, as I wait over the next two weeks, I notice things that I haven't before. At work one day a butterfly floats back and forth outside my window, high up above the roar and din of the city. In the park at lunchtime they are everywhere. How come I've never noticed them before in the middle of the town? Butterflies, I read in a book at home later, are about transformation.

I hope I am transforming.

The Powerhouse

So many questions,
a few answers.

We have arrived at the solar plexus chakra: the place where the mind and thought is processed. Here we can choose whether to ally ourselves with fear or with love. *Oh I know my mind lives mostly in the grip of fear.* Two weeks have passed since the last time the group gathered in the church hall. Outside, the sun is heating the day into a furnace. Inside, the air is cool as I catch up on news with some of the group before the workshop starts. Lots of us admit to feeling shaky. And so we begin our quest into this third energy centre. I learn there is such a thing as using my intelligence for soul purposes. This is in the realm of love. *What on earth does all this mean? I'm reeling around in this circle, unable to escape.* Jack asks us to write down three states to which we can aspire, together with the feelings we experience when behaving in accordance with our soul purposes. I can't understand the questions. I have no trouble naming three states I feel when I'm behaving nega-tively or three things I do to myself when I behave in that way. *I am depressed* covers them all. I look around to see everybody else writing furiously. I pretend to be making notes, rubbish, rubbish, over and over again. Deep despair, Jack tells us,

45

occurs when the ego is allowed to be totally negative. *So, my negative thoughts are part of my ego. That's another way of looking at things. They lead me to live in a state of fear; I'm hi-jacked by my mind's fear of everything; change, difference, anything new. My ego says I'm not important, I have nothing worth saying; anything I do, somebody else can do better; nothing I do makes any difference to my world; it's not worth bothering. But, maybe these deadening contents of my ego are a figment of my thoughts.* I know they are not going to be cast aside without a battle, for there is nothing else I remember about this day. I've written no more in my notes. What's happened to bring about such a lapse of memory?

I write about it at home later in the week after the workshop.

It strikes me as I look back through the long tunnel to my childhood that I don't remember having feelings about anything I did. The events are glimpses fleeing across a charcoal horizon; gruel lacking substance. Barren mountains stand blocking the way to the interior of the child. I allow some of the bleakness to dissolve. I can sense the child at junior school. She has to write about her summer holiday in Cornwall. *I'm bored with it. It's just a list of we did this and we did that.* What else is there that would make it interesting? How did you feel about it little girl? *Don't know. Can't say that.* So I meet the child's resistance to writing anything at all; it might be improper to write of something, which hints at how she feels. And that's what I'm thinking now. How can I write about myself, my feelings and thoughts? Nobody would be interested.

But I am.

I will linger by the light of a candle until some ideas emerge. I sit at the kitchen table and allow the strident chatter in my head to dim. It does slowly. *Remember the Introduction to Healing Workshop in May? Haven't thought much about what happened there.* I turn back in my journal and reread my notes. When I finish I hear a voice inside me, *where's the sense of wonder gone?* It seems to me that, in the time since then, my negative ego has been at work relentlessly debunking those rich experiences until I no longer believe they happened. Perhaps here is an explanation for my failing to write about the solar plexus chakra workshop. I have shown myself how this ego of mine strives to expunge any experience that does not fit with its negative view of my world and pushes me into depression.

What's the point of it all? Why bother?

Rage flames up inside me at times through the weeks following the solar plexus chakra workshop. It burns very fiercely when people ignore me, or talk at me. When they don't seem to listen to or hear me. I don't know what to do with its seething, writhing, exploding enormity. If I let it go, it will destroy everything in its path; it seems so out of proportion to what is happening in my outer life. One evening with a group of friends, it becomes so great I have to leave the room in the middle of an argument with a male friend before I blow up, decimating everyone, including me. Others think my anger very funny, I don't know why, unless it's to belittle me or maybe to hide their fear of fury. The volcano erupts again. My voice is blown away in ashes. I can't make myself heard, particularly by the man who talks at length with great confidence, completely unaware that anyone else, including me, has anything to say. He behaves as though I haven't spoken, when I have. He leaves no space for another's views. I feel I've climbed into a deep hole and cannot get out. I am obliterated.

Who am I, I wonder, this person who can't make herself heard? What is my essence? One evening at home I decide I'm going to write it all down in my journal. I'm a physical body, a female containing a womb, biologically different from a male body. This body has senses. Today the sun shines and my body feels its heat. The tea I'm drinking is warm, as it slides over the faint roughness of my tongue, tasting the sharpness and smokiness of brown fluid. If I cut my finger on a tin, its severed nerves feel the pain, the stinging of the open wound. I feel emotions. Today I feel sad, I don't know why. My thoughts say there's no reason to feel this way; but they mislead, because this is how I feel. I feel angry, but again my thoughts contradict; that's unreasonable or even dangerous. But these feelings are mine; they are not something I have been told about. They are telling me about how my inner world experiences the outer world. They tell me how I am different from another. No one can have my feelings and I cannot have theirs. My thoughts and feelings are my flame, my essence. They tell me when I'm tempted onto uneven ground, when I desert myself.

Heart's Place

**The heart chakra: the place
where we move from fear to love.**

If I can learn to love myself I will know how to love others. This is the fourth chakra workshop. It's two weeks since the last time we assembled in the church hall. It's beginning to feel like home as we chatter over cups of tea before we start the first session. The work is so intense each time we meet, that I feel I have known many of the participants for years rather than just a few months. My partner for this first exercise is looking into my heart. She tells me what she senses, someone looking in all directions seeking the right answers. This feels uncannily like what happens when I meditate. Always asking questions, looking for answers, not willing to wait, anxious to get past the chattering engine.

Jack tells us that in this chakra we meet unconditional love, love for the sake of loving; it generates compassion and for-giveness. *Ah, this is what the lady of India is showing me.* It will take a long time to reach this stage, because most of us have not learned about emotions at the solar plexus level. *Oh yes, these stored legions of rage and fear are what I'm experiencing now. But is love about allowing them to emerge? I might be beginning to make a little sense of how these centres of energy work together.*

As I meditate during the day on the dilemma of how I might find rest for my seeking mind, I see my thoughts as dancing stick figures, wilting under the onslaught of their ceaseless activity. Suddenly they reel in and wrap themselves in a shawl of gossamer fine wool, ready to be rocked asleep in my arms as a tiny dreaming baby. I must remember this.

♫

At home, a few days after this heart chakra workshop, I find myself writing mindlessly in my journal, 'Love is what I steel myself not to feel. It's a dangerous sword.' I stop writing as my heart constricts and then flutters; something is trying to leave or maybe enter. I close my eyes and see a pond of pale chartreuse water, frozen hard. The sun shines from a cloudless blue sky and, as I watch this peaceful landscape, melted water trickles away in small rivulets from the edge of the pool. But I stop the sensations, flattening spirit with deadness. Why do I do that? Maybe I don't want to allow myself to feel love so I needn't feel its lack. I sigh. But I don't want to be like that anymore. I want love for myself because, when it's absent, I experience an empty, fear-filled place where death lurks, lying as a weight of iron in my chest saying, *I am so worthless.* I've hidden these feelings for so long I cannot explain them; they seem without foundation. Yet they exist within me.

And so I sit at home in my quiet space and ask my imagination what stops me trusting that I could know the way to love

myself? An image appears of me, as a child. I am being smothered by a pillow. How can I escape from this? The lady of the
emerald sari appears. I hear her words. *It is time to cut the ties
that bind you to an old way of loving. You must stop trying to love
in the way you have learned; to be swamped with worry about others
and yourself. This is not what love is.* She slips away.

I write then in my journal. This is how my mother is. This
is how I am. And these words stop my writing and return
me deep into the ravine. I'm within the awful blackness of
my childhood and adolescence but I see nothing. There are
no sides, no base, no sky overhead to shed a chink of light. I
twist and turn my body and brush against nothing; I breathe
no air for there is none; no sound disturbs this airlessness
surrounding me; no recognition in my mind of what memories
are here for me to describe. As I tell myself this is all there is to
be experienced for the moment, the mournfulness for what is
unremembered overwhelms me. I cling to myself, waiting, as
some of the huge pressure inside me is ejected from my body.
This is a lone visit. No events of my life float before my eyes.
There is no clear image to catch. Only this place where there
is no sight, sound, touch, movement. I am being shown how I
must live through the fear until I can name it.

♫

The following evening, as I wash the dishes, fresh thoughts
float up. *Love is all about doing what others want, about not disa-*

greeing with them, being what I think they want me to be. If I say 'I love you' to anyone I will be swamped, taken over, smothered by them. I will have to become the person they want me to be. I can't say 'I love you' to myself, certainly not with meaning. I am overcome by lost trust, in myself, in anybody. I've never been trusted to know how to love. After finishing the dishes I write a letter to myself. It doesn't come all at once but in trickles, as I allow myself to hear what is in my heart.

Dear Me

I want to love myself enough, and trust myself enough so I can fly. How do I do that? By not placing constraints upon myself. By not saying 'yes, but…' By allowing myself to sing or paint or write without constraint. I want to love me such that I will come and sit at my side and tell me my troubles. I don't want to tell myself that my troubles do not matter. I want to tell myself, if I would be quiet for one moment, that I will hear the chimes telling me I have found myself. I want to hear what is in my heart not just in my mind. I want to hear me speak it without fear or favour.

I have to allow myself enough trust to do right for myself; in doing this I will do right for others. I cannot trap myself in a web of guilt and everlasting obedience. I say fly off and do what I will. I may get it wrong but who am I to say what is wrong. I will not allow myself to be smothered any longer. When I hear my voice, I shall listen. When I say I am frightened, I will listen and value what I have to say. But I shall also be full of the joy lodged in the creative womb even while

I open my heart to the pain lying in its craterous wounds. When I speak of my expectations of me, ask if they are mine or another's. I can no longer live the life that has been charted for me; it is not my life.

When I speak of what is in my heart, don't say 'I can't hear'. Don't pretend I speak in a foreign tongue that it is beneath me to hear. Just know that my survival depends upon being able to hear and accept me. And I will learn. What I ask myself to pretend, I must now be. For this is my life. Take off the ill-fitting borrowed cloak; it has served for too long. For if I do not, I may die.

Into the Blue

**When you're standing
on the edge of
things.... pause,
breathe slow.**

Kay Leverton

Another two weeks have passed since the last workshop and it's time for the group to move into the throat chakra. The trepidation I feel on these occasions hasn't disappeared. But some inner will propels me to return, as though drawn by an invisible skein running through a maze of my mind's roots struggling to keep me trapped. The focus of this chakra is all forms of communication. It is linked with the expression of truth and is the centre of trust in oneself, others, life and the Source. Its colour is blue. Jack says that when this chakra is blocked, it is not possible to express emotions such as grief, despondency, and hopelessness, nor buoyancy, lightness, hope and elation. Each time we don't tell the truth, we are interfering with the flow of energy in our bodies; we are not expressing the spirit within ourselves.

This hits home. I have discovered that as a child it was far too dangerous to tell the truth. If someone had told me there was a big notice in our household saying 'There is no such thing as anger, there is no such thing as fear', I would have believed them. Such feelings were not allowed. But I must have known them at some time. Now it's far too difficult to tell the truth about my feelings. A lot of the time I'm not even aware of them. Other times they feel too dangerous. I have a well and truly blocked throat chakra.

In a circle, taking our little child around with us, we dance and chant. I imagine her holding my hand. She's dressed in her first tutu. She insists we break out of the circle, even though I think we should stay. I feel her taste for the freedom of skipping and hopping in her own rhythm. I'm the little girl who jumps from cloud to cloud, singing at the top of her voice. Together we weave in and out, laughing, giggling, swinging around others, chanting words I don't understand until, out of breath, we sink slowly to rest on the floor.

As I wait for something to appear, I begin to feel sickness at the bottom of my stomach.

I can't get my breath.

I choke and gasp.

I sob silently.

This is death.

I sit on the floor. My body. Scrunched up. Heaves. Gasps.

After a while, Jack asks us to go to someone who is in distress.

I cannot move.

I'm suffocating, my breath locked inside me. It cannot escape.

Someone comes to me and then another. *I'm dying. I'm being smothered. I can't escape. There's no hope.*

At last my breathing calms. I return to the world and hug my companions as if this is my last moment on earth, wondering if I have just been to the place where grief and hopelessness, and buoyancy and light have become confused. They all seem highly dangerous. The message is 'Don't have fun and feel good because you will have to enter this very dangerous territory.'

Chapter Three

On Hearing the Child

Chapter Three

On Hearing the Child

By the end of the series of chakra workshops, I sensed that a three dimensional map had formed. It charted the territory through which I needed to travel to find answers to the questions "Who am I? What am I?" But it was indistinct and incomplete. I had kept no notes of the last two workshops, one on the brow and the other on the crown chakras. My hazy recollections told me that I made even less sense of them. So I had no neat package. But, I hoped that whatever I needed to remember had sunk into my body at some level.

Much of the landscape I had encountered felt hostile and demanding, but some was welcoming, where I felt at home. My task was to enter and absorb it, in order to know the child who waited in the distance of my interior. She had different voices, was different ages but, however she appeared, she seemed a stranger to me. She knew the scenery intimately though. Her secrets lay deep in the ravine where I had stumbled into stored legions of armed and dangerous forces. I felt overshadowed by their might. They were instrumental in keeping me locked in a place of inactivity. I had sensed, as well, some of the talents they guarded and, I knew that if I could nurture them, more might be revealed. But it was clear to me that I might have to descend inch by inch, to retrieve what lingered there.

The child spoke through my imagination; that is through my emotions, feelings and sensations, which are the language of the soul. This was how she could communicate to me, the adult who could choose to respond with love or with the fear of disbelief, disgust, dismissal. So a major part of my task was to restrain the power of my adult mind in order to allow feelings long buried deeply inside me, to emerge. At this time, I saw my mind as a fortress constructed higher and thicker during all of the years of my life. But unseen missiles were breaching its walls as I began to learn about the ways in which it had ordered my life, my beliefs about myself, about other people, about the world, so that I might survive. It was so reluctant to recognise any other ways of knowing; everything had to be subjected to reason, to cause and effect. It was filled with so many unnamed fears at the thought of encompassing my feelings, emotions, sensations. It didn't want them revealed, to it, to me, to anyone else. It couldn't cope with ways of knowing, through my hands, through my senses, that were not tangible to it. It was scurrying round looking for a way through a thicket, which had always been there but was now becoming visible to me. I had to free myself, to find my own voice but my mind was programmed by my terror of what would happen if I got in touch with it. What would be revealed? Somehow, I had to learn to make myself heard. Just what was it I had to say, about what and to whom?

Having heard the little girl on the clouds singing at the top of her voice, I wondered if I had ever sung as a child. I decided that I was going to learn to sing. Maybe this way would help me move through the thicket.

The Teddy Bears' Picnic

Through frost brown vines wait
black globes burgeon in summer
tongues taste burgundy.

I'm one of seven little girls, wearing a bear suit of thick brown cotton, dancing and singing my way to the woods to *The Teddy Bears' Picnic*. How many times do I lose my position or forget the words to the song? I don't remember. The only difference between our costumes is the colour of the inside of our fat, floppy ears. Mine are royal blue. I'm three years old and this is the first display of my performing career in front of the public. I have no photographs of this time, just a newly retrieved but fleeting recollection. Maybe it's one of my first memories. Perhaps this child has some connection with the little girl I've found in the base chakra, singing her heart out while dancing on the clouds. I feel her voice throbbing through my body until it fills my ears so insistently that I must find a way to free her. I'm going to have some singing lessons. *Quite ridiculous. What on earth are you thinking of at your age; you'll make a fool of yourself; never had a voice, couldn't possibly have one now; can't keep a tune in your head.* Well I have the 'phone number of a teacher who says anybody can learn to sing, so we'll see. It takes me half a dozen aborted attempts before I find the courage to leave a message on her answer machine asking her to ring me. When she does, I talk about my doubts. It will probably be a waste of time. But, at last, I commit to a lesson.

My very first lesson. I sing "oh, oh," and "ah, ah" up the scale and then down, as my teacher drums each of the notes out on the piano. Sometimes I go very fast, to get the feel of the whole scale without thinking too much about whether I've got the right notes. And, of course, a lot of the time I haven't. But I am beginning to get the feel of moving my voice up and down the scale. So, I learn that I have to start listening, so that I can match my voice to the sound from the piano. Slowly and carefully, I concentrate on hitting the right pitch.

But I'm hooked. And once a week I present myself for a lesson after work in the evenings. A lot of time is spent in trying to move my ribs out so the diaphragm can expand and power the breath from the solar plexus. I'm not used to breathing from there. But to sing properly, without strain, this is vital.

'Babies do this automatically,' my teacher says.

They don't raise their shoulders either as I do when I breathe in. This is another thing to stop.

'Relax them. Now let the jaw go.'

It is tightly recalcitrant. So much to learn, to let go of.

'The breath must support the voice,' my teacher intones.

Without it, the notes are flat, sluggish in reaching up; or sharp, overreaching, curbed of their fullness, weedy in space. As the weeks pass I begin to hear this. Without the breath there's nothing. I wasn't expecting this hard, physical work. And it's quite technical. And I discover I have a deep voice; I'm a contralto. I don't know whether I'm glad or sorry about this. There's something uncomfortable about it. It doesn't sound feminine.

During one lesson, while I'm singing scales, my teacher says, 'Carry on practising while I put some bread out for the birds.'

I continue.

'You have a very powerful voice. I could hear it quite clearly from the bottom of the garden,' she says when she returns.

It's quite a long garden and the double-glazed patio doors were closed. I am mortified. Now, not only do I have a deep voice, it is powerful. Is this feminine I ask myself? It makes me feel uneasy. There is a darkness about it. It's not how I think it is to be feminine, not dainty, flutey. It doesn't soar like a soprano's, which can be heard above all others.

In between lessons, I sing at home, sometimes, but not enough, up and down the scales and learning my first song. I've been having lessons for about four months and practising is the last thing I want to do one evening after coming home from a meeting in London. But I have to master my first song, *I Attempt from Love's Sickness to Fly* by Purcell, for my first performance in front of other people. It's not a major event, just a group of my teacher's students, which she has been asked to take to a small music group.

'I haven't been singing for long enough.'

'Your voice is developing nicely.'

'I'll forget the words. I might freeze.'

'Nonsense. It will be good for you.'

It's pointless for me to argue any more. The trouble is that as I continue to practice, I hear a singing voice inside me. *It comes from the distance across golden plains and craggy rolls of mountains. As it draws nearer I hear its uniqueness soaring, perfectly in tune. I am in harmony within it.* But I can't express it outside of myself.

What's stopping me?

♫

One day as I'm immersed in these early months of learning to sing, I'm stopped in my tracks by the sight of a little girl. She's about three years old, wearing a royal blue coat, its full skirt falling around her legs as a deep frill. She's dancing and twirling in front of a large mirror, swinging a scarlet scarf around her head. We're in a large store in the centre of the town, and workers like me are hurrying back and forth in the shortness of their lunch breaks. There's no time to wait and watch, but I do. Her face is alive with laughter, as she watches herself in the mirror, enjoying the movement of her body swaying from side to side. As I sink inside myself and feel her uninhibited pleasure in just being herself, I'm startled by a voice in my head. *You'll be sorry for taking such pleasure in yourself, you silly little girl. Don't do it to yourself. Don't lay yourself wide open like that.* An unbearable feeling of bleakness creeps through me as I wonder where the voice comes from. I move on my way, deep in thought. A woman brushes my shoulder as she rushes past. An electrical charge shoots from the base of my spine to the top of my head. The centre of my body is open and raw as though a scream has embedded itself in the membranes of my womb. Its echoes reverberate through the cavities inside my body, which continues to quiver.

It dawns on me gradually, as the weeks pass, that when I sing, the creative energy moving my breath through my body, has to power through all the emotions stored in my solar plexus. This is a cauldron stirred by a witch who serves up a potion I have difficulty in tasting. I have to stop singing. It's much too frightening. What I can't bear to remember closes me down. I'm so angry when this happens as it has tonight. I tell myself over and over again that I love myself and open my mouth. A very young me appears, so frightened that the adult I am now creases into a heap in the corner, shaking, gasping for breath, waiting. I'm back in the ravine brought here by the very song I seek. Can I colour just a little of the blackness? A writhing pain lodged within my body speaks just one word — shame. This is where singing takes me and this is where I stop, even though I don't hear the child's command. But I have to keep singing and so….

Persuaded by my singing teacher I join a choir, which comes together once a year for about two months to prepare for a carol concert.

'It will be a good experience,' she says.

This is where I struggle to find and keep my voice in the midst of others. But just before Christmas I find myself standing on the stage of St David's Hall in Cardiff, just one of several hundred, taking part in the concert. In the mass of singers I feel unsure of myself. I lose my voice unless I can be near someone who is firm in their pitching. For the moment I can hear such a person. I relax, allow myself to sing out. *Oh Come All Ye Faithful* is a familiar carol, but I must remember I'm a contralto; our line is not the one I know. I push my voice more confidently and feel it filling my body and moving through me. I'm enlarged by it. And... I'm about to spin out of control. I'm going to faint. I haul back on the controls; surreptitiously move my feet and toes to ground myself.

I'm still here.

A Taste of Bliss

If you can talk, you can sing;
If you can walk, you can dance.

African Proverb

Over the months I continue to build bridges of song between the adult me, the wounded child, the all-singing and the all-dancing girl. The hurt child is almost inarticulate. She makes it clear she's been ignored for so long she cannot speak of how she feels in words. I'd like to ignore these feelings; I'm making them up; I don't know what they are about, so they are nothing to do with me. But I cannot ignore them. They are in my body, with a reality much greater than anything in the outside world. But I find it very difficult to find a focus for my efforts. Most days I write in my journal, scribbling and scrabbling, looking for hooks of understanding, much in the way a rock climber searches blind for a new hand- or foothold. But I'm hardly able to distinguish between the child and me. I explode. My pen scribbles craggy shapes across piles of paper until it gouges down into the next and the next sheet of the writing pad.

My adult mind has such difficulty allowing her to speak. One evening I light a candle and imagine myself to be the girl of three and tell her over and over again how much I love her. She appears through my body as, one by one, my limbs petrify. She paralyses me. I know I've been at great pains to avoid this state for so long. Emerging, I hear a conversation in my head. *Don't moan about your unhappiness. Cheer up, nothing is that bad. But I know it is. I've just felt it. I can't ignore this. It won't go away. Talking about it will only make it worse. Just get on with things.*

These are some of the messages that lead my child to close down her pain. But I hope for something that might bring me some clarity. I can't give up.

♫

A few days later I sit at my desk at work one afternoon, thinking through some urgent problem. I have just twenty minutes to write a briefing paper. The office throbs with the sounds of activity. I pause, pen in hand to compose myself. A sensation creeps over me – one I've never experienced before. My body becomes light as though it no longer sits on its chair. My limbs are solid yet without weight. Like molten gold they mould into shapes of their own choosing, not mine. They know where, when, how to place themselves, without effort from me. I might not be my body. *Don't think about what this is. It'll only disappear.* I see the world illuminated from within me by tendrils of silver. It floats as a reflection in the meandering waters of a deep pool of magic. I don't have to do anything. I haven't been trying to feel like this. I wasn't aware it was possible. I sit here, being. I don't know the person who has mountains of work to deal with, meetings to speak at, problems to solve, worries to attend to. There's just this moment to be in. I don't know where it has come from. I try not to think or wonder *can I keep this feeling?* It evaporates, as water cupped in my hand must eventually trickle away though my fingers. For it will not be held. It disappears as mysteriously as it came. *There. It's gone. I've driven it away.* Is this how the little girl in the store felt? Did I feel like this as a child? Might I have known this feeling at some earlier unremembered age, in order to be able to know it now? If I could know how it came about I might be able to bring about its return.

For days my thoughts are filled with this gift of nirvana, a taste of what might be. Perhaps a place inside me, which is saying, *yes I'm on the right track for myself.* Maybe the moon can help me find that place again. One evening, at home, when she is in full flood in the indigo sky, in my imagination I visit her. As scudding clouds set her free in her pearled nakedness, I draw her light into my body. Her white energy seeps from chamber to chamber and rolls her way down to below my navel. A great blackness filled with chaotic figures appears. They will not identify themselves. My thoughts are overwhelmed by something unknowable to them.

The next day remembrances flash by of times as a child when there were no feelings of bliss. The dancing display when I end the routine out of my place. I'm six or maybe seven years old. I don't know how it's happened but in my white tutu, with red and blue ribbons in my hair, I'm at the end of a line of little ballet dancers in a place where I've never been in all the times we've rehearsed. I'm usually in the middle of the line because I'm the tallest. I'm afraid of the dancing teacher. She shouts a lot. I've arrived in another place. I've forgotten myself. I play the piano at junior school for morning assembly. I'm about nine years old. Halfway through the hymn I don't know where I am. There is a vacant space where once was the piece I knew so well. I begin again. Another day in my first term at Grammar school - I'm eleven years old. I sit gazing at the cherry trees set in the neat acid green lawn outside and smell the geraniums in a box on the ledge below the open window. A hard sharp pain startles me. It's a piece of chalk hurled by the teacher. It's hit me on the cheek. So that's why I don't like the smell of geraniums. I wonder what I was dreaming about? I write these memories in my journal.

And then I ask the question. What does my child feel about these events? For a fleeting moment, my stomach shrivels and the stench of humiliation spreads up to choke me. My child makes some important decisions. She gives up playing the piano, dancing, daydreaming. She closes down a part of my life she knows is too dangerous to live in.

The day following these remembrances, a small figure appears, a golden light shining in the darkness. *I'm here. They didn't want to know me. I'm the best thing that's happened. They don't want to hear from me. I disturb things too much. I can't get through to anybody. I have to do everything they want, when they want. I don't want to sleep when they want me to. I don't want to stop playing when I'm supposed to. I don't want to get up when I'm meant to. I daydream when I should pay attention. I don't want to eat what they say I have to. In fact it's like I'm not here.* Her voice is filled with outrage. It's a life of endless compulsion.

Some days after the appearance of my child, I'm having Sunday lunch in a pub with friends. My attention wanders to a family at another table: mother and father, with three daughters. The elder two, who look to be about nine and seven, are blondes; the youngest, about four, has chestnut hair. This could have been my family when I was young. The two older girls are playing with their father, shouting, laughing, and vying for his attention. As one clambers on to his lap, the other squirms under his arms to wedge herself between them. They wrap their arms tightly around his neck and fight not to be disengaged. As their squeals and shrieks reach a crescendo, mother shushes them. The youngest, who sits quietly next to her on the padded bench seat, is still. Her eyes slide back and forth watching from afar every move made by father and sisters. Eventually she loses interest and, from the pile of clothes next to her, she draws out her mother's long, brown coat. She slips to the floor, dragging it with her and dresses herself in it. She totters a few steps, the thick woollen cloth trailing behind her, before she is pulled back and divested of it by mother. It's time for the family to leave.

The scene plays over and over in my mind for weeks. I tell myself to stop thinking about it and a ball of rage unrolls its way through my arms and legs as it struggles to escape the confines of muscle and tendon, which would capture it in my throat. It says. *I'm that youngest daughter. There's no room for me with my dad. I'm desperate to join in the games with him. My sisters have taken up all the space. There's nowhere else to go except to stay quietly at mum's side.* I am being shown how jealous I was of my sisters as a child. I'm shocked, for the adult me has never been aware of such dark feelings for either of them.

♫

The singing voice I hear inside me whirls me on, though its effortless dimensions will not appear from my throat; but what does appear, is growing in timbre. My teacher thinks it will be good experience for me to enter a singing festival. I have about four months to prepare three songs, one each for three different categories of the competition. I begin work. My teacher records, on tape, two versions of the piano music for each song. One has the piano accompaniment and the song line. The other has just the accompaniment – this is all I will hear on the day. I use these tapes at home to practise. Learning the notes, where they are on the stave, getting their pitch just right, bar by bar, over and over again. Alongside this work with the music, I learn the words of the three songs; one German, another Italian, the third English. And kind friends correct my pronunciation. Then I bring together the words and music and it's like beginning all over again to learn the songs. Each weekly lesson is taken up with going over the parts of each song that I find the most difficult; because of their intricacy; or because I want to breathe in the wrong place; or I cannot breathe where I want to because it spoils the line. All the while I am hoping to make the songs I have chosen flow inside me as seamless rivers in all their moods and colours.

The day arrives and the first competition is about to begin. I'm sitting in the Banqueting Room of the Guildhall in Bath. I am trapped. The only people present are those taking part in the competition and their supporters. The morning outside is sunless. Three huge chandeliers hanging from the pale green, domed ceiling are lit and glittering in the gloom of this nine o'clock morning. I'm number six on the running order. I wish I could go somewhere to warm up my voice with some scales but there is nowhere. I immerse myself in the early performances; my nerves must not have too much space to cause havoc. The first person is singing. I know without any doubt. I am out of my league. *I won't think about that now.* The second competitor is on the stage and she sings, as I know I cannot.

My teacher whispers in my ear, 'These people travel around the country entering competitions. They are experienced.'

Why does she wait till now to tell me? What am I doing here?

'I'll be back in time to hear you,' she says as she disappears.

The next three people are not present. Have they decided it's all too much? I am called to the platform. No time to prepare.

I will be all right. I walk forward my heels clattering on the wooden floorboards.

Heads turn. Faces say we don't know her; she's a new one. From a deep recess inside me a voice says, *you are absolutely on your own; there is no one here you know.* A void opens into which I am ready to fall. But I cannot go there. I pack it with disbelief and close it. Climbing the steps, my feet wear leaden weights; my knees knock with a hollowness that must be heard everywhere in the auditorium. I feel no pain. My stomach revolves with the frenzy of a merry-go-round ready to hurl itself from its circle. The accompanist takes my music, speaks and looks enquiringly at me. I see her mouth move but hear no words. I nod. She shrugs. I turn and compose myself but it's an impossible task. I cannot relax. If I do, my body will dismember. Behind me portraits of Queen Charlotte and King George III look down benignly on me. Below me, the judges sit at their desk, pens at the ready; they are expectant. Beyond them row upon row of seats, most unoccupied, wait sightlessly. I fight my deepest desire to flee from the stage, and announce the name of my song *An Die Musik* by Schubert. The first notes on the piano, once so familiar, are unrecognisable. I open my mouth hoping instinct is bringing me in at the right place. The first few words emerge, trembling offerings tottering from the shadows. There is nothing to follow them. My breath has ceased. Nothing in my solar plexus moves. The tunnel of my throat is closed.

I wait as the piano accompaniment drifts out over the judges' heads to the ears of the empty rows. My legs shake, the right lifting off the bare boards. I look down; the foot is attached to me but no amount of effort will keep it in place; it taps away aimlessly.

If it had its way I would not remain here on this stage.

A complete line of black and white notes passes as I struggle to reveal my voice.

It reappears, stays for three lines then retreats to its self-imposed exile.

With a will of its own, quite out of my control, it makes one last appearance to offer some of its colour and power. It is over.

This has been no nightmare. It has been a living mare. I stumble from the stage shaking like a limp aspen tree. Something very powerful, which I cannot hear, will not allow my voice to be heard.

Weeks later I dream.

I look through a window of my childhood home. The red brick wall edging the back garden bulges and winds along the thin lawn. Tree skeletons bend; the wind howls through their branches. They stand firm. Flashes of lightning turn night sky into haunted day. Thunder reverberates, wrapping itself in rolls of chalk grey. One gigantic knife of silver light hurls itself out of the anvil sky to strike a building beyond a fence. Shattered glass flies through the air and I shout to my mother that the house over the way has been hit. Steel blue smoke curls into the sky. From it, a woman emerges leading a young girl of about nine; she is dumb. I wonder if she is simple. The woman says she has brought her to me to be looked after. I wonder what to say to the girl. As I look at the house the entire rendering on the outside walls has fallen away, leaving bare brick showing.

The thunder and lightning feel very much how I experience my life now. Thoughts whirl like dervishes, trying to escape from whatever it is I can't bear to touch. But I must hear whatever it is my child has to tell me even though she does not have the words. Memories are packed into every cell of my body, not just as words recognisable by my mind, but as bodily sensations containing clues to what is really important. Often it's the seemingly smallest and silliest things, which are the spark; messages in words I don't remember hearing as a child, but they light up old embers. So I have to watch for times when this happens in the present. Such as the day when my mother is nagging me to clean the family silver, which she has bequeathed me. If I don't, she says, she will take it back. Without warning, a forest fire out of control sends flames racing through my body, rising from the pit of my stomach to the crown of my head, burning to ash whatever rational thoughts lie in its way. The speed of it makes my body want to rise from my seat, to burn like some brilliant meteor in the sky before disappearing never to be seen again.

'Fine. I didn't ask for it.' I actually dare to tell my mother how I feel about something she has said.

She laughs, 'There's no need to be like that.'

So this is one of the ways the child learns not to trust her feelings. She is wrong to have them. She deserts them; buries them; pretends they never existed. Their memory fades and disappears. This is how she learns to look after herself and her mother, who also does not care to deal in strong feelings. She has to be the goodest, most obedient girl. She is omnipotent, certain she can make everything OK by ensuring that her hurt and anger don't come flooding through.

Chapter Four

Can You Hear Me?

Chapter Four

Can You Hear Me?

I was learning that the physical act of singing drew breath up from deep within my body to follow the path of the chakras.

Childhood secrets held as blocked energy in the base, sacral and solar plexus were being pushed from their dark hiding places into the light of the heart and throat chakras, which were prepared to witness whatever I would allow myself to communicate to myself. But there was only so much I could manage at a time. This process was liberating energy, which was beginning to express itself through my body and feelings, rather than being restrained by the judgements of my solar plexus mind. Of course there was no wholesale ejection of all negativity. But I was discovering that each new step forward meant that yet more of my previously unrevealed beliefs emerged to be inspected and jettisoned. The contents of the ravine still needed to be challenged.

I decided I needed to help myself listen more deeply to myself and I joined a counselling course, one evening a week for a year. I didn't have any idea of becoming a counsellor; I had a full-time job. The emphasis of the course was on acquiring and practising the skills of listening, hearing and reflecting, and on developing empathy. Towards the end of the course we were asked to identify a 'problem', not a major one, for a series of sessions each week. We would be counselled by and would counsel a colleague, the aim being to practise bringing together all the skills we had learned on the course.

At the beginning of the following year, as I embarked upon the next stage of counselling training, my mother died. My account of her last days opened this book. Though our relationship had been troubled often, much of the year was filled with mourning her. Just before she died, I was invited to join a newly forming Women's Group. The task we set ourselves was to explore the nature of the Feminine. In the early meetings I was doubtful about being there. I felt uncomfortable, but I wasn't sure why. We continued to meet once a month, at the time of each New Moon, over a period of three years. I quickly discovered that my child felt so bad about some aspects of being a woman that she would prefer I didn't belong to the group. Hence my resistance. But it was as though the death of my mother had in some way freed me to dig deeper into the child's secrets. From here on I began in earnest to explore the nature of Feminine energy and this became an important focus of my continuing search for myself.

Through all this time, singing remained my constant companion.

Golden Girl

**Between one place
and another there is
always room to grow.**

Kay Leverton

I dream.

Watching Woman has the eyes of Hawk seeing every detail from her place by the gate at the side of the field. Full moon floats in black cloudless skies casting her light over the scene, making silver of trees, hedges and grasses. The wind whines and bare oaks dance a minuet to their own eerie music played by groaning limbs. Standing Woman stoops to take something from the inside of her car. She lifts her head to catch the eyes of Watching Woman. There is a moment of recognition and a shot rings out. The body of Standing Woman lifts into the air, hangs like a rag doll for one shocking moment, and falls to earth. She lies as a crushed heap of bones. Watching Woman sees what is left, a golden silk jacket lying on the ground. She looks down and sees a shotgun resting in her hands.

She knows she has shot a prostitute.

I'm struggling to describe my dilemma to my counsellor at our first counselling session. It's not a major problem. 'I've been developing new interests, particularly since I attended some chakra workshops more three years ago. But I don't know which I want to pursue most. There's not time for them all. I have a full time job.'

'And your job is?'

'Well I work in the Civil Service. I write briefings for Ministers, and draft replies to parliamentary questions; attend meetings, write guidance for local government and health authorities. I manage about ten people. Stuff like that.'

'It sounds like a responsible job.'

'Yes I suppose so.'

'So what are the new interests you're thinking about?'

'Well I've passed one singing exam. Do I want to study for another or throw myself into a choir? I don't think so, but I do want to sing. Is there some other way I can use my voice? I want to turn my journals into a book about my quest to heal myself. It'll take an awful lot of effort. Even if I do manage to complete it, I don't know whether I could ever get it published. Would anybody else be interested? Shall I continue next year with more counselling training; do I want to be a counsellor?'

'You have a wide range of choices,' the counsellor says.

'Yes I suppose so. They all feel much more inviting than my job.'

The counsellor waits.

'I'm disenchanted with it.'

Where does that come from?

'I didn't know I felt like that.'

'Can you focus on this feeling,' the counsellor suggests.

A whiff of boredom arises from a well of disenchantment. Words bubble from it.

'Well, my career's been my life, but the intellectual challenge doesn't satisfy me any more. I'm not interested in most of what I have to do. It never used to be like that. The buzz of excitement's disappeared.'

This is shocking.

'I've never dared admit that before, even to myself.'

'All the things you've identified you want to do, are creative pursuits. I wonder if you feel in need of a change of career?'

What on earth makes her think that's what I want. No, that's not my problem. It's about choosing which things I'm going to do in the time available. I'm not thinking about giving up my job.

Our time is up.

Before the next meeting, in my course journal, I write up my reflections on the session. My stomach begins to toss itself around. How on earth did we end up talking about giving up my job? The counsellor's got it all wrong. But maybe she hasn't. Dare I think about it? What if I find I really want to give up my job? Could I make that happen? If I think about it, get attached to the idea and it doesn't happen, then where will I be? I couldn't go back to not wanting to inhabit another world. I would be even more unsatisfied. I wouldn't be able to hide behind the pretence. I'll have to make a decision I'm afraid to make. Oh, now I remember the list I assembled, a few weeks ago one evening in the group, of my self-defeating behaviours and thoughts. I can't change anything because 'they' — that's just about everybody else — have the power. I can't make up my mind because I'm not sure what I want to do. Then, there's no point in being confident because I'll surely get it all wrong and I'll look a fool. Or .... there's no point in doing this or that because I won't be able to do it; whatever I have to do must be "all right" otherwise it's "all wrong"; there's no room for mistakes here; it's dangerous to experience my feelings because I can't do anything about them. Oh yes they're all here at work with me now.

But, I can't let events carry me on as they have in the past. So what does my job do for me? It gives me money to live on, a sense of a secure and safe place. My contribution helps me feel worthy. It's more than that though. It's how I identify myself. If I give it up, I won't be able to earn enough money for quite a while – to keep me going until I get a pension.

How did I get into this?

I sob over the words as I recognise that whatever else has been going on in my life, my job has been my refuge, my place of safety. It's been my home where I can hide myself, where I can live in my head. But it doesn't work any longer. I've many more parts to myself. Is this what happens when I listen to myself with empathy, when I hear what's behind all the usual excuses for inaction? I'm not sure I want to know about it.

No I don't want to change my career. I'll tell the counsellor at the next session that she's got it all wrong. It's not what I'm thinking of; it's too scary.

But the kinds of security my job gives me are proving to be something of a chimera. The child says the world of feelings is a dangerous place. It's too painful to express myself creatively. That's why I went to live in the world of my intellect. This is where I feel safe; it's my home. I've made it part of me and I've become it.

This place of security is a myth I've been burrowing into without realising that's what I've been doing. I'm now facing myself with the fruits of my efforts to change. It's no good saying I never intended this to happen. I need to go through it and trust that wherever I come out will be right for me, the person who I am rather than the one I thought I was meant to be. I can't pretend any longer that I don't know what I want. I have to find out.

In the next session with the counsellor I describe how thinking about giving up my job — putting it under the microscope — is like discovering that I've been in a relationship with someone whom I've cared about deeply but I'm beginning to realise we don't belong together any more.

I hear my father's voice in my head. 'A good education and a worthwhile job, providing security, are what matters.'

To write, to sing, to counsel do not qualify as life's work. That's what I think he would say were he still alive.

I feel like the prostitute in my dream. I've been selling myself as a person who I think will gain approval. In doing so, I've betrayed the real me. But her talents, I feel, are tainted. I pick up the golden silk jacket from the earth and place it around my shoulders. I slip my arms into its sleeves and settle into its sleekness. I have to learn to love its sensuousness and vibrancy.

Women's Talk

Shoulders hunched
a shrouded woman
lours and moans.

A letter from my child.

they got the cat killed the man drowned it it was bleeding if you bleed you get killed it's no good you cant bleed and live you have to die it's not fair why does the man kill it it was a nice little kitten it was black and soft and velvety it had to die cos it bled it's not fair why did it have to be killed because it bled it was nice it was ok it was pretty i liked it it was soft why did you kill it if you bleed youll have to die somebodyll make sure you die hell strangle you with his hands in the water no question why couldn't she live that mans big hands killed the little kitten why didnt they tell me she was bleeding id have looked after her she'd got a collar id make sure shed be ok they never even told me til it was all over they never told me what they were going to do I want to kill them who says they can kill her i could have saved her theyre cheats she was our kitten she who must be obeyed did it she let it be done she's horrible why cant you bleed and still live theyre not safe people not the man next door nor my mum and dad he wouldnt hurt a flea and he gave the kitten to the man next door to kill don't ever bleed.

♫

I trap thoughts sneaking through my head. *All this talk about menstruation, bleeding, childbirth, children. This is nothing to do with me. I don't want to touch it, hear it, speak about it. Why on earth do I want to be talking about things like this? I don't want to be in this women's group. I want to be a different kind of woman from this one; I want to be without this blood and stuff. I don't want to glory in all the pain and bleeding. And children, what's so wonderful about having them? They'll be smothered just like I was. I'm not going to continue in this group. I've worked hard all my life to escape from all the monthly pains and humiliating menstruation. What's the point of sitting round talking about it? I'm not going to talk about it, think about it anymore.*

But, this is part of being a woman; it's part of who you are; you cannot reject a part of yourself whether you like it or not. This is why you're in this group; you must get to the bottom of these feelings if you are to be the mother to your child.

I sit quietly and calm myself. I concentrate on my breathing. In and out, the breath moves. It takes me into my physical body to the solar plexus. *There's a huge boulder here. I'm going to shift it out of the way; I make no impression on it. It's stuck, lodged in the middle of my body. I put my shoulder to it, this huge lump of grey granite; it's blocking the opening to a cave. There, I've started moving it.* My head moves back and up and around. Heat begins to grow inside me. It fills my body and shame leaks into blood. I am the child.

How do I feel about my periods? I don't know.

When do I have my first one? I don't know.

How old am I? I don't know.

Where am I? I don't know.

What **do** I remember? The Curse. That's what it's called. It brings pain, discomfort, inconvenience, sticky messiness, smelliness, embarrassment, secrets, hiddenness. Just the cursed curse. Take some pills, keep going, pretend its not happening. No celebration, no cherishing. Just endure it. Tears pour across my face. Too late to celebrate. I can't stay here. My womb is weeping. Too late.

I am full of grief, in these months following the death of my mother. I miss her in many ways, some I never imagined. After all the years filled with worry about her, there is a space where I find it missing. When she was here, I felt needed in a way that I no longer do; there is a gap in my life. The relief is not as I expected. She has left without telling me about something I need to know. How did I come to feel so bad about being a woman? I know she didn't have the answers; when she was here, she couldn't fill in the gaps for me. She didn't remember telling me about periods, or when I started them. She felt sure my two older sisters would have told me. Nobody remembers. I, to whom it happened, don't.

But the way through does open. In a quiet, meditative state, I write to my young child. Secrets, hidden from me for more than forty years, begin to emerge. She responds, in her letter, in a direct, explosive way, full of outrage and terror from deep within the recesses of my body. I begin to understand why she has appeared to me before as paralysed, mute and helpless.

She speaks of the fate of the cat and kittens. I have only a shadowy remembrance of a cat in our family at some time when I was a child. That is all. Shortly after I receive the letter from my child, my eldest sister, Annie – six years older than I - comes to stay with me. I ask her if we had a cat when we were young.

'Oh yes, don't you remember?'

'What happened to it?'

'We'd been out somewhere one day. When we came back, the cat – it was little more than a kitten – had had kittens. They were all taken away and destroyed.'

So this event is not some figment of my imagination. It happened. I wonder how old I was.

My sister works out that she must have been about nine.

'So, I would have been three.'

My adult mind says this is a very small incident, quite unremarkable. But the sheer weighted enormity of the terror pouring through me in the writing of the letter, tells of the disappearance of that child's trust in her parents. They arranged to have the kitten she loved killed. How could she be sure they wouldn't do the same thing to her?

A few days after the first letter, another emerges from the child who is about nine or ten.

im on the bus im bleeding im going to die what's happening i hurt in my insides it hurts in my body im dying help me im dying help me im dying help me isn't anyone there im dying and no one knows what have i done please i don't want to die will i get home before i die please don't let me die no one knows im dying im going to die please please it hurts why do i have to die im not making this up im not it's all black how will i know where they take me why isnt my mummy here im all alone tell me im not going to die nobody's heard me they won't notice what is this blood the cat died i can't help bleeding maybe it was ok it needed someone to hear it god bless the cat the middle of my body hurts

A few days after receiving these letters, I dream.

I'm in my kitchen. A cat jumps over the heaped dishes on the draining board and jumps through the window. It falls behind a wooden trellis against the wall opposite. I try to reach it. It's a little boy. He's trapped, maybe dead. I call to a friend to come and help me rescue him. As I reach him, he's no longer an infant but about nine years old. He's not afraid; he's really wild, shouting 'Get me out of here.'

I have a huge healing task on my hands. At times my child's experiences feel so remote from me, as if they were those of persons who lived long before me. And I've shown myself how, as a child, I lost three lives.

The physical – as far as possible I have attempted to ignore my physical body all my life.

The emotional – I have made a monumental effort to bury all my feelings other than those I think of as positive.

And the spiritual – I have denied any relationship with a God and I have no faith.

I have survived by taking up residence in my mind. I set out on my task of re-membering this child. I write copious letters to her, answering her concerns, praising her for her courage; accepting everything she has mentioned; telling her how I would have dealt with each episode. I reassure her I understand all her feelings and tell her how I feel about her. I offer her all my love and protection. This is not an easy task. The adult me so wishes to fulfil all my tasks but I can go only so far in re-parenting her. She still feels so distant from me. Sometimes I'm an inadequate parent, at other times a completely intolerant one. I don't know what are the right, loving things to say to such a traumatised child. There are times when thoughts of getting closer to her feel repugnant. How can it be that what I most long for, to hear a loving word truly meant, to feel a hug enveloping me from myself, is so difficult? The thought of loving this child feels alien. She's not worth loving. I must not condemn her but somewhere inside me I do. I try to draw closer to her but I don't wish to be so near to her deaths. For that is how they feel. I seal my letters with her and my tears. She knows how she survived. I have to convince her that her way doesn't work any more. I need to find ways of showing her how it's possible for things to be different now.

Chapter Five

Finding Jewels

Chapter Five

Finding Jewels

My child's fears about her bodily functions had thread their way through into the adult. I decided to name her "Claudia". I had no idea where the name came from. It was as though I had plucked it from the ether. Some months later, I discovered that the name Claudius meant disabled. I decided that the feminine equivalent was appropriate because much of what lay in the ravine had disabled "Claudia". She had so much fear, sadness and anger stored inside her that she was unable to allow me to change. But if I could help her to express these emotions then the energy that was used to keep them buried could be liberated. I continued to listen to her, to draw her nearer. It was she, I felt, who contained the essence of the Golden Girl. I was sure it was her voice I could hear inside me. If I allowed her, she was an adventurous guide to and from my interior; prepared to take up all sorts of opportunities that began to present.

I had started to learn about some of the ways of Native American spirituality – Shamanism – at weekly meetings led by Jack Angelo, who had facilitated the chakra workshops I had attended nearly four years earlier. I was attracted to Native American spirituality because it is not a belief system but is a spiritual path to knowledge. This led me to attend a retreat, "Walking the Red Road" held by Jack at a healing centre in Surrey. The Red Road is the way we walk this life on earth; the Medicine Wheel the circle of power, which can bring knowledge and understanding of all things. I've come to think of The Wheel as a path, a way of making discoveries about the Universe and myself; who I am, what I am, why I'm here and where I'm meant to be heading in this life. It teaches the balance and relationship of all things. It can stimulate our own thought, intuition, seeing and feeling processes to inspire us to come closer to our own soul and spirit. And, because it is circular, following the seasons and the directions, we travel around it repeatedly in order to learn from the lessons presented to us. Should we ignore them, then more and yet more opportunities will appear until we get the message. Sometimes we never learn. Everything in the natural world, creatures, rocks, trees, plants, the earth, the sky and each of the elements is our relation with much to teach us.

My experiences on that retreat led me to delve into the power of sound healing. This was a type of healing that I had never heard of before. In the spring, I tasted a few workshops in the UK, where I learned to chant, and to sound tones and direct them to the energy centres that I had learned about on the chakra workshops. I also managed to find, in a local bookshop, just one book on the subject. It was *Healing Sounds* by an American, Jonathan Goldman. I wrote to him asking if he was to hold any workshops in the UK or Europe. He sent me a flyer for a Healing Sounds Intensive he was holding that summer in Colorado USA. I debated with myself the pros and cons of going. Golden Girl was very keen, but "Claudia" was painfully hesitant. At last I booked a place. I went to Colorado to take part in the Intensive. There I was to learn about how the sound of the voice or of instruments could heal the emotions.

During the spring I had stopped having singing lessons. Though I had discovered that I had a singing voice, I decided that I wanted to explore other ways of singing. I had no idea how I was going to do that. But towards the end of the year, I saw an advertisement for a Voice and Movement Course in the UK, run by Gilles Petit. It sounded different and so I enrolled. And I was taken into my singing voice in a far deeper and, for me, more meaningful way.

Leading up to this period, I applied for early retirement and after waiting on tenterhooks for about eighteen months, I left my job in the Civil Service. I was about to become a counsellor and to learn to write creatively and to continue singing.

Mistle Thrush

**If you listen, really listen
you might hear your heart sing.**

I meet my Goddesses walking along the Red Road. I've a number of goals for this three-day retreat. I want to know more about what love means for me. How do I know the Source? How am I going to manifest my feminine power? How am I going to walk in love? And, where does the next bit of my path lie? My need to move towards these goals is heightened because the decision is made. In a few months, I'll be changing my career.

The South is my first step on the Red Road. It is the place of the healer, the lover and the child. My task for the weekend is to bring more healing love to my child, who lives within. Through healing my emotions I can come to find the trust and innocence in myself. This means embracing yet more of my personal history, and letting go of its negative effects, which still have control over me.

I am one of twenty-four participants, none of whom I know, assembled in a large room in an old house, a retreat centre, set in large wooded grounds in Surrey. Outside, the wind blows and rain scatters on the windows. I still don't think of myself as a healer, but everybody else here is. I sit on an upright chair in a large circle and Jack asks each of us in turn to introduce ourselves and place an item, which he has asked us to bring, on the altar.

This first session is barely underway and I feel bad tempered. I catch the edge of my thoughts and draw them nearer. *I don't want to be here. I don't want to have to fit into another set of beliefs like those of my childhood. I've left behind the Roman Catholicism of my early years. I do not want to fit into another blueprint. Everybody seems so sure of themselves. They seem to have all the answers. There's all this talk about the healing power of love and I don't want to be here.* Oh what huge resistance. I'll just have to sit with it yet again. I watch as people place their belongings carefully. Some bow or genuflect, and my stomach sinks. Irritation unwinds into dread. *I'm not going to kneel. I had enough of that as a child.* I lay my stained-glass dragonfly on the cloth. It usually hangs in front of my kitchen window at home. I see it every time I wash the dishes. In the Native American way, anything that can improve our connection to the Great Mystery that is life, is known as medicine or healing. Creatures, plants, rocks, crystals, the winds, the rains — all have patterns, habits. These can show their messages of healing to anyone who observes their lessons on how to live. Through my reading I have learned that in calling upon this colourful flying dragon I am seeking to be drawn into harmony with the strength of its essence, which is to do with transformation. I discover now, from Jack, that its particular vital energy is about transforming illusions. This gives me another way of looking at its medicine. Illusions are habits created by my mind. If I can spot them, I can change them. My resistance – perhaps it's a mind created habit – retreats for the moment.

The effects of my patterns of thinking become a little clearer when our dreams are placed under the spotlight. During the first night of the course I dream. In great anxiety I'm searching for my heart. Although I am rushing around looking in each room of the large house I am staying in, I don't know how to find it. An enormous sense of loss and loneliness for something unnameable creeps through me. And I wonder will my home be burned down when I return to it in a few days. In the circle, the following morning, we share our night time revelations. I recount my experience and find myself wondering out loud why I hadn't been able to say I was a healer, as everybody else on the course had, the previous day.

'Maybe,' someone says, 'It's time to admit you are.'

Could I do that, I wonder? As I contemplate the statement 'I am a healer', an enormous feeling of relief creeps through me and I unwind my body. It is sufficient to think the thought for me to feel differently. I don't have to do anything else for now. For the moment, I know that whatever other irritations crop up, I am meant to be here. In another's dream, I recognise the polluted waters into which he has to dive repeatedly to clean them as something I need to do for myself. The waters of my life are polluted still by habits of thinking about my feelings as being negative. I have to continue to dip into them in order to transform the pollution.

Later the same day, I discover how pollution can draw me nearer to its insistent familiarity. I'm on a walking meditation in the wooded grounds of the retreat centre. It's raw, cold, blustery as I plod along the earthen paths, head bent, shoulders hunched around my ears, wondering how I could know my hearted-healer better. *Right, just allow that thought, straighten up and enjoy being here.* My body unwraps and I begin to stride through the woods. Gusts of wind whip crumpled leaves into a frenzy before lodging them in the straggling undergrowth. Trees stand ready to receive spring's signal. Amongst the chattering chorus, the song of one bird penetrates through the mist-shrouded afternoon. At the top of a windswept, bare-branched beech a mistle thrush sits, repeating its six phrases again and again. They echo high through the moaning boughs, insisting I stop. I draw the music nearer. The trills enter me and reverberate through the chambers of my heart. As its song revolves there, I feel no separation between the voice of this bird and me. It has become mine, it is ours. I dance in circles along the paths, nurturing the repeating chant close within my body. I reach the far end of the grounds, and the sound fades. Now it is lost to me, drowned by the deadening roar of traffic on the motorway lying just beyond the boundary. I am drawn, with insistence, away from the song of the mistle thrush. The bird hasn't flown, but I can't hear its sound or feel it in my body any longer. What am I doing here when I could be away from this noise? I retrace my steps. The birdsong returns.

Is this what happens to me? Does my voice become lost, polluted by the noises of the world? I can choose which to hear. Maybe in life I choose not to hear the song in my heart. It feels like I don't have a choice, I can't escape the sounds of the traffic and so I'm powerless to stop its invasion of my being. But I can. My heart is recognising a link between the sound of song, healing and love, which I don't really understand. There's something missing and I need to find what it is. The next morning I'm introduced to the power of the drum as we greet the day. As I hold and beat Jack's drum, I feel a call from within of an ancient rhythm, which anchors me to the ground. I have a fleeting feeling of coming home. I am at rest in my body.

Before we leave the retreat, Jack asks each of us to find a tree in the woods, and leave with it some aspect of our lives we want to let go of. I walk outside. Can I do this? Can I leave behind some part of me that's so familiar, even though I don't want it? My crippled child, "Claudia", swims into my mind. It is she who has been disabled by the pollution of negative thoughts. She doesn't want to appear in public and will do as much as possible to stop me exposing her. So she appears apparently unbidden, as I try to transform myself. But I want to save her. If I give her away I won't be able to. But I don't want to be her anymore. Will this help loosen her hold over me? Deep in turmoiled thoughts, I set about finding a suitable tree. If there isn't one then I won't leave her. I hunt feverishly. Show me the right one please. Maybe that stout oak is the place. I run my hands over its rough bark before leaning into it to drink its strength. Once it was a tiny acorn. How many years has it taken to expand to this size? My arms won't reach around its girth. *Is this the right one, "Claudia"?* I close my eyes. She unlatches my limbs, turns me around, and walks me through the ferns and shrubs. *This is it.* I open my eyes and lay my fingers on the silvery bark of a slender birch, shimmering in the arriving dusk. The mistle thrush sings its evening song from the topmost branch. I give "Claudia" into the keeping of this tree and bird. How can I do this? I still I don't understand how she became so crippled. She feels so dear to me.

Somewhere inside me, I know I have to leave her cradled in the arms of silver birch for her to reveal yet more of her secrets.

Boulder

I'm standing on the edge of the Rocky Mountains in Colorado. Far below in the distance lies Denver, no more than a hazy sprawl of dark shapes spread on a pale beige plain. It's just before six o'clock in the morning. Seven of us are waiting for the sun to appear over the horizon. We've come together at this time to sing to the rising sun our intentions for the day before us. I allow whatever tone my body wishes to make sound into the pale orange globe, as it climbs before me into the expanse of fading indigo sky. I ask for forgiveness for myself and for all those who I feel have harmed me.

I've come to this part of Colorado, above Boulder, to take part in seven days of total immersion in healing sound. To learn and experience a whole range of exercises developed for healing people. It's an exploration of how making and receiving sound can affect mind, body, emotions and spirit. Witnessing the rise of the sun each morning is not for everyone but, for those who choose, it's followed at 7 a.m. by a healing circle at which, most days, there are between six and twelve of us present. We take it in turns to stand in the centre of the circle and be bathed in the sounds of our companions' voices. One morning, I allow the delicacy and strength of the others' toning to bring forth my tears and be comforted by the sounds as they fill and surround me. I feel as I imagine a baby does when held in comforting arms.

It's taken me several months to decide to come all this way to learn about sound healing. My experience of the song of the mistle thrush and leaving "Claudia" with the silver birch is helping to unlock my need to experience much more about the ways in which I can explore and use my voice. By the time I pay my deposit for the course I am filled with a certainty that this is the right thing, in spite of all my fears shrilling, *what are you doing? This is madness.* But two months before leaving, I do begin to wonder if I will get to Colorado. My aunt, my mother's eldest sister, falls ill. When it becomes clear that she is to die shortly, I wonder how I can leave her. But then the doctors tell her that she has a matter of a month or so to live. And so, with her usual determination, she sets about dying. Within three days she says her farewells and leaves. Two weeks later I fly to Colorado.

I am one of thirty people gathered in the large room of a wood-built hut set in the Rockies. We sit on elderly sofas and chairs set around the room. The sun outside burns down and inside this room it is hot and airless. Participants have arrived from Germany, England, Wales, Holland, Canada and from many parts of the United States, including one man who has ridden his motorcycle from Wisconsin.

'Took me best part of two days,' he tells me as he shows me his immense machine.

'It's like an armchair,' I say.

'Sure is. And travels just like one.'

The leader of the Intensive is Jonathan Goldman, a teacher, sound healer and chant master. He sets out the domestic details. All our meals will be provided, except on two days when we should group together in fours to buy and cook our meals. He also reminds us that, as we are nine thousand feet up in the Rockies, we need to drink plenty of water to avoid altitude sickness. Introductions on the course come by way of ceremony. Jonathan asks each of us, in turn, the name by which we want to be known during the course; the colour we want to work with, and our intention for the nine days. Three days before leaving for Boulder, full of anxiety about the adventure, I decide to see if I can contact any spirit guides I might have. I'm not aware of having any but I am learning that I can access their wisdom, if I choose. By writing with my left hand, I hope to get in touch with my intuition, bypassing my active mind. I sit in the candlelight.

'Who is there? Why have you come to help me?'

A spirit speaks. 'My name is Freya. I live in the North and I will be your guide. I see you with dark glasses in bright sunlight. I will help you to see. You will need to go underground to connect with your understanding of human nature. Let things flow through you and much will be revealed.'

I don't know who Freya is, but I have a vague idea she might be a goddess. After a great deal of searching, I find a book about Norse mythology and there she is, the Goddess who sees the souls of the dead over to the other side. I have no idea what all this means for me. But on this first day of the course I remember her name, and decide this is how I will be known for these days of sound healing. Everyone tones "Freya" and I'm bathed in the sound of her name, surrounded by the colour magenta as I make, within, my intention to work with trust; to trust myself, to honour my own experiences.

Harmonics quickly become the focus of attention for all of us on the course. Normally when we hear a note struck or sounded we seem to hear just a single note. But actually a mixture of a number of harmonics or overtones are created. Whilst we can't individually distinguish them, they contribute to the overall colour of the sound. We spend days practising and learning about the effects of toning – using the voice as an instrument for healing. With vowel sounds such as 'oh', 'eee', 'ah' we learn to resonate each of our chakras, helping to bring them into balance. Every spare moment, on the slopes of the mountain, we practice stretching the vowels slowly, turning 'uh' into 'eh' waiting for the overtones to appear eerily high above the pitch of the note sounded. In the bathhouse as again we practice, somebody breaks wind; it has its own overtones in this tiled building.

One morning, all thirty participants begin the day's work with sounding our world into creation. We beat drums, blow horns and didgeridoos, tap tambourines, ring bells, shake rattles and, of course, sound our voices. The only constant in this work of creation is the beat of one drum. Otherwise we have no instructions. I close my eyes, ready to meditate.

One soft beat echoing the throb of the heart enters the silence, and pitch black slips into leaden grey of dawn. Water lapping around my feet rises in white mist while, with faint thuds, shoots of tree after tree emerge from bare earth to grow noisily through steam. Faint breezes spring up as each branch sends leaves out ready to applaud the arrival of the creatures of the jungle. Creakings and rustlings become squeaks and grunts and conversations of the wildlife get underway. Rays of sun penetrate the now heavy green foliage, capturing flashes of turquoise, emerald, crimson and yellow feathers of exotic birds, as they set up their insistent song. The warning snarl of a leopard cuts across the lines. Wound round the trunk of a twisted tree, a silver and black snake sleeps, oblivious as an elephant trumpets its greetings and warnings. I'm sitting in the centre of this wilderness, drumming, making and answering calls with my voice in this newly created world.

We come to rest at the end of an hour, our task complete. I am filled with the beginnings of my new life.

One evening, after supper, we spend about two hours blowing twenty-one Peruvian Whistling Bowls. The originals of these modern, moulded clay vessels with spouts date back to 500 BC and were used by Andean cultures to facilitate healing, open spiritual doors and enhance shamanic experiences. The sound they make when blown together can help access those parts of our body where there is blocked energy, leading to its release, balancing, healing and deepening a spiritual awakening. Jonathan explains that this will be the first time, in his experience, that so many vessels will have been sounded at the same time. As we blow the bowls, they make a high-pitched whistle. It pierces my skin like tiny pinpricks before moving deeper into the flesh below and setting my teeth on edge. Gradually, way below this high-pitched sound, I hear a low continuous moaning wind, travelling from ancient times to seep through my bones. Part of me wants to run as far as possible from these sounds, which I no longer hear through my ears but feel in every part of my body. It's a relief when we stop. Jonathan suggests that we make a note of any feelings, sensations, dreams that we experience overnight.

Later, six of us from my bunkhouse lie out on the mountainside watching stars shooting way above us. They seem much nearer than at home. Well, we are nine thousand feet up in the Rockies. But it's not safe to sleep outside; bears might be roaming, so we retreat to our bunks.

During the night, my sleep is fleeting and filled with dreams vivid with colour and sound. I am driving along a winding road in a red car while an unknown man smoothes my hand. I know that three people are dead: my mother, aunt and someone, who seems to be me.

In another, I'm visiting a town and know that a very important person is coming. I see the station where banners of welcome are strung around the buildings and across the street. A band is playing and crowds of people are waiting for a prince to arrive.

I'm woken from this dream. It's 5.30 a.m., time for the sunrise ceremony. I roll out of my bottom bunk and double over with a wracking pain in my right breast. It radiates through every part of my body. *Those Peruvian Vessels have a lot to answer for.* I struggle down the hill with another sun-riser; she wants to get me to a doctor but I know a healing of some kind is taking place and that I'm the doctor. For this morning I will have to miss toning the sunrise.

In the shower I stand under the hot water and focus on the centre of the pain in my breast that I lost to cancer seven years ago. I have no choice but to allow old grief I've been unaware of pour out of me and wash away. The sobbing moves deep into my body and erupts as a geyser springing out of the earth. Not for the first time I know that grief is not a far call from madness. It has no thought of reason attached to it, it just is. It becomes a river in flood hurling aside the great boulder of my resistance flowing wherever it needs to at great speed, heedless of any obstacles. It knows when its force is spent. It meanders to a halt. I can't imagine that I might have drowned, but later, this is what my mind thinks could have happened. Going with the flow is a reality. I emerge from the shower to find that one of the women, who shares the same dormitory as I, has stayed in the shower next to mine waiting for me. I hug her thank you for caring enough to allow me to go where I needed to with freedom.

Throughout the rest of that day and the following days I notice a lightening in my mood and a greater sensitivity to the sounds I hear, to the country I see and to whoever I'm with. Sometimes though it is not comfortable. Remarks, that would not have bothered me before, hurt. Misunderstandings seem to arise more often. And I find I need more space as feelings of yet more sadness begin to emerge.

Meeting Magic

We are eleven plus two teachers in Trinity Chapel in Bristol. It is a Saturday in October. These three days are part of the ongoing Voice and Movement course I've embarked upon with Gilles Petit. Each of us is exploring what our sound feels like in our body using the names of the notes of the Indian musical scale, 'Sa', 'Re', 'Ga', 'Ma', 'Pa', 'Da', 'Ni', and top 'Sa'. I allow the breath gathered in my diaphragm to support the first, 'Sa'. It's the same note as the drone playing on the harmonium. I unloose strained muscles into new places of holding without strangling and settle the 'Sa' into my body. The sound rests on earth warmed by rising sun. I allow this home note of the scale to bed low into the centre of my body as it travels into nooks and crannies between the vertebrae of my spine. A purple plain, over which the sun spreads its orange glow, settles around me. This 'Sa' rises into the caverns of my mouth and out into the world. I listen but the ground beneath me, the walls around me do not return it to my ears. I repeat it and cells of my diaphragm implode as strings, held firm for so long, stretch into new places. I touch my jaw with my hands to feel strong bands delay the note as though something new, hidden might escape with this 'Sa'. It falters and stretches palely to meet the light of day. A new breath and it powers from within and I feel it sink into marrow and blood. I have engaged a sound more bedded in my body than before. It is mine, speaking of an ancient place within that is only dimly remembered. My task is to find that home again and again. I hear it, sometimes above, sometimes beneath other voices around me travelling to meet and return to my ears filled with the experience of its external journey.

I wonder if I dare move to 'Re'. Never mind about all the voices around me. The feeling in my throat and mouth of making the sound of 'Re' is so different from 'Sa'. It's an in-between note, a question even. I'm taking a lift from the ground to first floor, and stopping off in between. The location is at the back of the tall thin building of my throat. *Can I find it? Here goes. This feels right, where I feel the vibration contained on a narrower shelf in my mouth. Explore and fill out this sound. Feel comfortable in it. Don't think of moving on. Don't allow it to slip up or down. It's not a plateau like the notes above and below it.* So I settle here for a while, exploring this elusive sound until I'm ready to move to the third note.

It's 'Ga'. Here, the sun rises in its round glory; it lights the grey morning confident of its place in the firmament. I feel it sure and steady; it is resplendent as it surrounds me. Now it disappears into the shade as my throat and jaw tighten. *Relax. Take another breath.* I start again and feel the warmth of the 'Ga' grow into its full expectancy; it knows there's further to go but it's replete in itself.

The fourth note, 'Ma', sounds like its name, the eternal mother. *How do I reach it? Where must my breath touch the chords; which shape inside my mouth will bring it into being? Where does it lie in my body?* I launch my voice but it's not found the place of safety. I seek, I question but there is no sureness of its place above the confident 'Ga'. *Is this it?* I hope it is.

I move to 'Pa'. *This feels like a home; a secure place in the arms of, like its name, a father.* I fill this sound out around me and hear it reflected off the walls of the chapel. I might stay here but I could reach up to its neighbour.

'Da', the sixth note cracks. It's too high. *But I've been there before. I know I can again. Oh head, you can't tell me about this. I have to feel it.* I'm no longer sure what I'm doing.

Let's go back to 'Sa'.

Here it is.

No I've lost it. I can't find it.

I listen to the other voices and they invade me.

I am parted from my voice. I can't find the place in my body from which my 'Sa' comes.

I put my ear to the harmonium and listen. *Is it this or this?* At last, I find the note in my body. For a while comfort rests here. I sing it over and over again feeling the sound as it unwraps old folds in muscles and invades the shrouded crevices of ancient caves. These places creak into my consciousness waiting to reveal their memories. My confidence grows enough for me to leave in search of other notes of the scale. I hear my voice meeting with others, becoming entangled for a while and then separating to go on its own journey until….

I'm lost again.

I stand, silently agitated, seeking my place within. I'm distracted by others' voices. They become mine. I creep into a corner, testing for my 'Sa'. The pathetic mewing of a kitten is all that emerges. Waves and waves of other voices blot me out. I cower, hands over ears listening to my stomach winding itself into gurgling knots. My breath leaves my abdomen and rests in my throat, panicking. I cannot inspire or expire. I am immobilised, drowning in wild sounds.

Once, I asked my mother what I was like as a child. One of the two things she told me was that when I came home from my first day at school all I could talk about was the noise. Perhaps my body is remembering that day now. There are twelve other people in this room and I am invaded and killed by their voices. *I no longer exist.* I've read somewhere that we each have our own sound but this is the first time I have known the truth of that statement. I exist as a sound but if it is overwhelmed then I can die. To be filled with someone else's sound, which is foreign to me and in which I can't hear my music, smothers me. Chaos and the void meet head on, each becoming infected by the other. Is this how my silence becomes contaminated?

In the midst of my bedlam, I stand to make a sound that keeps me anchored. Someone near to my ear sings it back to me. It's Gilles' voice. Through the din I hear him say, 'That's 'Pa'. It's magic.'

'No it's too low for 'Pa'. I know I'm not there."

'It's 'Pa' below, not above, 'Sa'.' He leads me to the piano and plays the note I've been singing.

I can't find it. I start again from 'Sa', taking my voice down to 'Pa'. *Yes, here it is.* I settle my body around it, allowing it to expand out of the back of my throat. I'm surrounded by and immersed in it. Here is peace and security. There is no effort for me as it makes its way from deep in the cavern of my womb. It is a light but bedded rumble and feels as if it might travel infinite distances with no effort. I let go of the note and pick it up again. The sound exists even when I can't hear it, waiting to be carried on the wind as the waves break on the shore whether or not I'm there to hear it.

Chapter Six

Alchemy

Chapter Six

Alchemy

Gilles had told me that the sound of 'Pa' was magic but I couldn't feel it even though I was making it. I longed to know the magic of my own voice. But I had experienced, in different ways, the power of sound vibration to enter my body and seek out and dislodge reservoirs of energy trapped in cell, blood, bone, muscle and cavity. Surfacing on that rising energy came the pain of buried memories to tell their stories. New expanses appeared from which my ancestral voice was beginning to emerge. As my lighter and emptier body engaged more fully with its sound, I began to be challenged when moving in front of fellow members on the Voice and Movement Course by yet more old messages. *Who do you think you are, showing yourself like that? That is shameful,* emerged from the space and silence. I took these voices home and slowly challenged them to rest. It was no easy task for they operated often through my body, freezing it into a mass of indecision. When they did emerge, rage, sorrow, relief and even joy accompanied them. But I was beginning to understand that in the Native American tradition, each time I circled the Wheel and learned whatever lessons I was capable of hearing, I reclaimed new territory. And I was led to dig even deeper to find more of the impacted roots of outmoded beliefs and messages.

While this work continued, I was invited by my nephew, Andy, my sister Sue's younger son, to his wedding in Mauritius in the summer. Evidence that I was changing, getting more adventurous, was becoming more open to challenging myself, came when I thought, *Yes I will go, and what's more, I will stop off on the way home in Zimbabwe.* I had dreamt about returning to Africa ever since I had first gone there thirty years earlier. I joined a safari to Lake Kariba and Hwange National Park. First stop was Kariba, an inland sea 175 miles long, created when a dam was built across the River Zambezi. It was completed in 1958, flooding the valley where fifty thousand Gwemba Tonga people lived. They were moved to live in angry exile in one of the most inhospitable parts of Zimbabwe. Over time, the level of the lake had fallen as a result of drought over nine consecutive years. From Kariba, I flew to stay at a tented camp outside Hwange Wildlife Area. The National Park covers over five and a half thousand square miles. I discovered that Hwange means "Peace".

From this journey in the outer world I brought back powerful images, bridges to my interior landscape. I was helped in experiencing their significance by joining, in the autumn, a year's writing course "Women Writing Autobiography and Short Fiction" run by Cardiff University. I had spent so many years in my former job writing official documents – reports, speeches, briefing for Ministers, guidance on this and that, drafting answers to parliamentary questions. Writing fast and to order, clarity and conciseness were of the essence. I needed to free myself to write how and about what I wanted to. My mission was to find my writing voice. I had the idea that I wanted to convert my journals into a book. I knew, too, that the process of producing a book, whatever its fate, could help take me yet deeper into the 'Who am I?' question.

Kariba and More

Arrivals Hall, Harare International Airport, Sunday, 5 p.m. and I'm standing next to a pillar, trying not to be an anxious traveller on her own. I want to be the shaman and the writer for the next two weeks, observing, absorbing and recording as much as possible of the country, the people and the creatures. The luggage carousel is wandering aimlessly across the shabby concrete floor. People with empty trolleys jostle for position at its edge. Like racing cars on the starting grid, each is determined to have pole position. Some operate in pairs, the front man maintaining position against all-comers, his partner manoeuvring the waiting cart behind. The first case lurches from a black tunnel to set off on the next stage of its journey. It remains in stately progress alone until joined by more of its companions. The rush is on. Somebody's ankles are horribly suitcased as a man ducks and dives with his belongings, oblivious to all. At last I spot a green bag. It could be mine. Edging forward, I insinuate one shoulder between two men, intent on their own business, and slither into a forward position. I judge speed and angle, making ready for the lift. But no. It's too tall, too sleek. I retreat to my pillar. A man, in impeccably cut, dun coloured shorts and shirt, is organising a similarly clad group. Above his tasselled socks stretch marble white legs. These travellers look as I imagine newly arrived European colonialists might have, fifty or more years ago.

I'm resuming a love affair with Africa even though it's thirty years since I was last here. I don't understand the chemistry of the romance. It might be something about an ancient land, the source of the original humans who migrated to populate the world; the wilderness and the eternal fight for freedom. I remember from my teenage years and early twenties being absorbed by the battles in Kenya and later Southern Rhodesia, now Zimbabwe, for Independence. On a different scale I hear echoes of my own battle for liberation, throwing off the yoke of a tyrannical ruler.

The hall is emptying fast and new cases are appearing less frequently. *Perhaps mine is lost. Do I mind?* In spite of my best efforts to pack essentials only, I can barely lift it. Attending the wedding in Mauritius meant I couldn't scrimp. That's what I tell myself. I feel my mood lifting at the thought *my case might not turn up. I could travel light.* But, here it comes, the last one, dusty, battered as though it has been rolling around in the African earth. I reach out to pick it up but a porter beats me to the draw and whisks it away.

'Follow me, please'. He seems affronted that I could think of managing without his assistance. 'How long are you staying in Harare?'

'Just one day.'

'While you are here, you must visit our National Gallery to see the stone sculptures of Zimbabwe. They are acclaimed around the world.'

We emerge from the gloom into bright sunshine and I spot a woman holding a board with my name on it. She's from the holiday company through which my trip has been organised. I tip the porter and say goodbye.

A taxi takes me from the airport into the centre of Harare, named after Chief Harava, along roads lined with jacaranda trees heavy with pale violet blossom. Crushed blooms cover the red earth beneath with a thick mauve carpet: a marriage of heaven and earth. The sun, an overweight orange globe, lights the horizon with crazy bands of scarlet and purple. By the time I reach the hotel, the heavens are navy blue. The moon has swallowed the sun. Dusk is missing in this part of Africa. I'm staying at Meikles Hotel, on the corner of Third Street and Stanley Avenue where it's been since 1915. Although it has been rebuilt since then, it still has the feeling of the colonial period, when it was the original hunter, farmer, prospector's hotel.

The next morning, I set out to find the sculptures. But it's Monday, and the Gallery is closed! The Sculpture Park is open though, and I wander through the Garden absorbing the round and elongated stone Goddesses and Gods created by some of Zimbabwe's finest sculptors. Zimbabwe means "Houses of Stone". The first Zimbabweans were the Stone Age nomadic hunter-gatherers known as San or Bushmen. Along the crowded streets at the centre of Harare mine is the only white face abroad. And nobody seems to notice…except the street sellers proffering strange wire models of motorcars.

The following day I return to the airport for the flight to Lake Kariba. I'm staying on Spurling Island, but because the level of the lake has fallen over the years, it's now joined again to the mainland. That afternoon I join six other people to see some of the wildlife. Dust rises on the hot spring breeze as we bump along a rutted track. The end of the dry season is near. Impala interrupt their grazing of sparse scrub to lift their heads and scrutinise us before dipping to continue feeding. They've decided that we're no threat. But something seems to be. The leader, raising lyre-shaped horns, springs weight-lessly into the air. This is the signal for the herd to scatter in all directions, skittering, ducking, diving; flight, not fight. In effortless leaps they rush, weaving through and over bare bush, round slim trees. Coming to a stop, they gather together in a pow wow. Is the threat real? Must they continue to flee, this time in better order? Whatever that one impala sensed hasn't materialised. They resume their grazing. Four zebra, their former companions, remain nearby grazing contentedly, stolid and sturdy in their hazy striped coats; white, the masculine light by which all is made visible; and black - the feminine, wherein lies what is hidden.

It's nearly five thirty and our ranger has spotted a lioness, way in the distance. We near her as she lies under a Mopane in front of a small copse on a slight incline. In the sinking sun, shadows are long and she's surrounded and camouflaged by the matching orange land. A companion lies on the other side of the tree, sunning herself. Between the two, a cub jumps up, curious to see whatever has distracted it. Within minutes another female emerges from the small wood. She strolls across to join them, bringing with her two more young ones. For a moment the pride rests together, elders forming a triangle sheltering offspring at the centre. One cub reclines against its mother's back, its red tongue lolling in the air. It is exhausted by the exertions of the journey through the bright sun of the scrub to the shelter of this tree. Another jumps up to play with mother's tail, until the game becomes too boisterous; she flicks the child lazily. It sinks down onto its haunches plotting its next escapade. One lioness gets up and moves a few yards away from her companions, looking off into the distance. I follow her gaze. She's intent on watching the hazy lakeshore. It is almost six o'clock and the pride is well placed to see visitors to the water. With so many mouths to feed, she may be hoping to surprise an unsuspecting imbiber coming for an evening drink. Eyes are almost shut against the still dazzling sun; mouths are open as lungs inhale and exhale dusty air, pushing sleek backs up and down. A breeze blows our way carrying their cloying, pungent scent. A period of pleasant relaxation is really the beginning of an evening and night of activity with food top of the agenda. Almost out of sight, a lion relaxes in the midst of the copse waiting for the females to do their hunting work.

Next morning it's five o'clock and in the time it's taken to wash, dress and have a cup of coffee, black night has slid into grey dawn. A lion's fresh footprints appear on the track we are following. I hang over the side of our vehicle tracing the prints until, after many miles, they disappear into dried grass. Further along the trail, a collection of bones lies in thick dust away to our right; all that is left of a bull elephant, dead of a slow paralysis of unknown origin or maybe of poisoning by toxins gathered in the receding waters of the man-made lake. Surrounding the remains, fresh prints of other elephants come to mourn their fallen comrade during the night just as they have every night of the year since his death.

By mid morning, we are floating on a pontoon on Kariba, sweltering in the heat and humidity. The locals say the weather of the suicide month, October, is early this year. Under the deepest shade of a canvas awning, we drift on the shimmering water opposite the shore. A herd of buffalo graze on the spring green grass near the edge of the lake. Their massive shoulders coated with water glisten as the untroubled beasts stretch as far as the eye can see. One fine specimen, stately horns curling up from the top of his head adorned by the most carefully coifed head-dress, watches us as we watch him. Sheltering from the sun in the shade cast by his muscular body, an egret, white feathers impeccably groomed, stands alert, awaiting its feast. Further along the beach, a grey log slithers with no sound into the water. As we edge further from shore, floating heads, sleek, wet and golden brown emerge through the ripples. Eyes set on the sides of skulls just above the surface of the waves, watch. Long jaws emerge to snort at us as we float closer. One hippopotamus opens her huge mouth in what might be a body-snapping yawn or maybe she's warning us not to come any nearer. She patrols a petrified forest of leafless trees, ghostly sentinels to past secrets. Trunks, worn smooth as velvet by lapping waters, startled out of their green mantles by floodwaters forty years ago. All that now remain are these sad, proud skeletons, stripped bare and risen from the dead. Yet more ghostly shapes lie in the deeps, ready to emerge again to face the burning sun. These standing sentries, exposed by retreating waters, are the resting places of the white and chestnut African fish eagle. It's "kiow-kiw-kiw" rings out across our heads as it sights its meal and dives. Many of the inhabitants of Zimbabwe are of the Venda tribe, who in turn are descended from the Shona tribe, and believe that this eagle is in touch with the world of spirit. So its Guano has special powers.

My three days at Kariba are over and I fly to Hwange to stay at Chimwara Camp, outside the National Park. On the third and last day here, I am up at 4.30 a. m. Nine of us sit, in misty dawn, around the embers of last evening's campfire, drinking tea and coffee and eating toast. We are to spend the whole day in the Park. Four hours later we reach our breakfast stop deep in the heart of the bush. It's quiet. No other humans around and the only creature to approach us is a glossy starling for its fill of crumbs. We press on to stop near a water hole. All seems peaceful until a herd of blue wildebeest appear in the distance, looking ready for a drink. Each time they set up a canter, their leader heads them away from the hole. What on earth is going on? Ah, on the far side of the water lies another inanimate log, a crocodile.

In the early afternoon, siesta time, we bump and sway over crusted tracks pushing deeper into scorched scrub. Vincent, our constant guide and driver, is intent on getting us somewhere to see something.

'It's a surprise,' he says.

I scan withered trees and dried bushes, watching and waiting. It's hard to believe that in a few months everything will be luscious green again for a while. There are no animals to be seen at this the hottest part of the day; but vigilant Vincent points to a group of black and white African Hawk Eagles perched knowingly in the uppermost branches of a towering monkey thorn far away. *How does he manage to spot them without binoculars at this distance?*

'They've probably sighted a kill and are waiting,' Vincent announces.

We breast a shallow hill and judder to a stop. Below, a hundred metres away, a deserted water pan gleams in the silence of the space between the notes of a song. We stop and wait and wait.

'What are we waiting for Vincent?'

'Wait and see. Just be quiet,' he whispers. He shrugs full of glee. He is of the Shona tribe and likes to tease.

At last. Sounds of splintering bark and branch herald the arrival of a lone elephant. With one final uprooting of a shorn tree she heralds the coming of the herd. Through the screen of bushes and tinder dry trees at least a hundred mothers, grandmothers and children emerge to sway their way towards the water. For the young, this is not just drink time, it's thirty minutes of hi-jinks with a purpose. Several young bulls join the fray and shower each other before rolling in the mud in wild trumpeting abandon. As the herd moves off, they trot in pursuit until driven back to make their lonely way into some other part of the wilderness. Within minutes, silence re-establishes itself. They might never have been here. We are about to leave, when a giraffe arrives at the water. It splays its slender legs right out to the sides. At such an angle, it looks as though they might break. It is drinking,

'The giraffe is very vulnerable like this,' says Vincent. 'A lion can attack by jumping on its back.'

We cannot stay any longer. It's a long, bone-shaking drive to leave the Park before it closes.

With dusk approaching, we arrive back at camp and settle on the deck at the side of another waterhole. The sun is thinking of sinking behind the trees, leaving gilded mud and sparse water. A great white heron stirs from its resting place as though to entertain or be entertained by our small group. It takes its place, with much fuss, opposite us on its stage, the remains of a fallen tree lying exposed in the shallows. Back and forth it struts with hunched wings and mincing steps, much as a high wire artiste in a circus of one. At any moment it seems it might perform a somersault but is beaten by the fall of darkness. Wanda, the camp's warthog, living up to her name, is sweeping and snuffling, with great dedication, the ground in our vicinity. She threatens one person, to whom she has taken exception, with a half-hearted mini charge. The fire is alight in the pit, its wood singed smoke spiralling off into the darkness. The waxing moon relaxes on her side in the star-littered sky.

Vincent is in his place at the fire. He's nearing the end of his stringent training to be a safari guide. No matter how deserted of creatures the landscape has appeared to be over the last few days, I've come to know the signs that he's seen something, which none of us has spotted. As the vehicle idles to a halt, he shares all his information. A giraffe loiters behind tall trees browsing on the topmost leaves. I've been looking at it but haven't seen it.

'The giraffe has a very large heart. You can see this in its eyes.' Vincent giggles. 'Look at the long neck. The giraffe needs such a huge heart for the blood to reach all the way to its brain.'

On a misty early morning drive, a pack of rare, wild dogs streaks across the scrub, way in the distance. I can only just make them out with binoculars.

'The most persecuted wild creature in Africa,' Vincent announces as we bounce over rough track. 'This is a rare sighting. Make your donations to the save the wild dog campaign when we get back to camp.'

Now Vincent's perfect teeth and the whites of his eyes glisten in the firelight though his face is lost to the night. He chuckles and is ready to tell another of his stories. This time it is "Why the Elephant Grieves".

♫

These African scenes return home with me and grow images from within.

I place my ear over bark worn by waters, left smooth and silken grey. Here I stand through centuries of seasons strong in all my glory as, lashed by December's wild winds, I bow and dance my wild waltzes. In sweltering sun my shade makes shelter for families of drowsing humans and beasts. I trouble no one. I need no books to learn, no professor to lecture me, no one to say 'shed leaves, they are not good enough'. I contain the essence of instruction within. From without, all I require is the loving nurture of the earth, the warmth of the sun, the light of the moon, the water of the rains. The change of season is sufficient to tell me when to rest, when to grow.

But one day, a storm gathers and sweeping, churning waters engulf me to my highest branches in a slow death. I am bathed and stripped of all that is me. I grow no more. I take my memories of all that has been with me. What have I to tell you now as you see my ghostly remains, a reminder of what once was?

I touch a grey trunk to hear the song. My body poisoned by toxins of unknown origin. Year after year I return, looking, yearning to know what happened. Unable to leave, driven by unnamed force to locate, to name, to make known. You show me that I must swim the waters to know the ruined shadowy remains lying submerged below.

I take up my pen to write into these images.

Opening Secrets

Air, warm and weighted down with water, metamorphoses before my eyes into swathes of transparent silver oil. Enveloped in this fluid, a bee moves from bloom to bloom humming with contentment, as it investigates for nectar with gentle but thorough intensity. It wastes no time in lingering where the cupboard is bare. Its progress is stately, methodical and it is in no doubt of what it is looking for. If not here at this moment, it will be at the next or the next. "Opening Secrets" is the title on a blank page in front of me for a piece of about 2,000 words for the next writing workshop. Take autobiography and turn it into fiction. I can't imagine where to start. In desperation, I make myself sit in the garden and wait.

Mr Bumble appears untroubled by the prospect of searching hundreds of tiny purple flowers on one bush. I wish I felt like that. Instead, a voice of authority sits inside sounding off like a drill sergeant on the parade ground. *Forward march. Right turn. Left turn. Halt. Listen. Writing is a luxury. Who would be interested in your experiences? This is no way to spend your time. And, hear this. What makes you think you can write?* I am fed up of hearing your voice. Silence.

'Do you believe in God?'

The question booms down the years from nowhere to expel my breath in one great wave from my centre. Whose voice am I hearing now? Ah, it's my sister, Sue, a few months before she died seventeen years ago. It is the first line of my piece. I'll talk to myself and to Sue and see where it takes me.

Pushing my sister's wheelchair through the busy streets of Tenby to this place at the edge of the harbour has stretched my muscles from their foetal curves into screaming cords held by fine tendons of steel. Up and down kerbs, I've navigated pavements hiding inclines up and down or, most lethal of all, sideways. People have given the chair with its passenger a wide berth, averting their eyes as they move around us. It hasn't been just because of my erratic steering. Eyes have slid a split second before bodies moved around us. I know some of Sue's friends at home haven't been able to acknowledge what their eyes have told them. I wonder if there's an ancient fear implanted deep within them too. I know it's here in me. It has no words but it started to grow from the moment I knew that my sister was so ill. It's a fear I can't name but whenever I feel it writhe within my stomach and fill my head, it urges me to run without mind to some other place. But there's nowhere else for me to go just as there is, for now, no other place for Sue to go. Has she seen the invisible cordon, which the dedicated holidaymakers have drawn around us, a boundary they could not cross? Were they embarrassed, shocked to feel their knowing of an unknown fear when they saw the chair occupied not by an elderly cripple but by a young woman?

I gaze into the harbour's murky waters made pewter by sunlight rippling over its surface from between the first renegade clouds of the day. Though I search through my mind for the words to answer my sister's question, my heart tells me no one has ever asked me the God question before. Or if they have I've never truly thought about it. I feel somehow that the answer's always been assumed, certainly by me. Do I believe in God? I don't know. I don't know what to say. Actually I don't want to have to reply. I want to be the young child I feel myself to be. To run to the nearby beach and bury myself up to the neck in sand just as we used to do as kids. I swing my legs rhythmically out over the harbour wall as though to propel me on that journey. I don't even know who or what God is let alone whether I believe in him. And why do I think God is a he? I can't bear to reveal the extent of my unknowing to Sue, not here, now.

Into my memory creep scenes of endless discussions at University lasting far into smoke-filled nights. Clutching glasses of warming beer, our small group of philosophy students debated, at first importantly, and then with greater and greater abandon, the meaning of life. Is there a God, who was Jesus? None of us admitted to a belief in God. Always there was the unspoken thought that to do so would be a sign of weakness, of a need that's too childish to be allowed in that place of mature learning. I have never thought since of asking myself these questions. And now, as I write this, I see with sudden insight that the debate never moved out of our minds into our hearts. I have felt ambivalent about God for as long as I can remember; the need to have an answer for myself has never seemed to figure in my list of important things, until now. That's right, there is no God; that's how it's been for as long as I can remember. Really? But I so want to believe there's something called good that's everlasting, making it worth inhabiting these frail bodies. That's fanciful I tell myself; I want to flee from any such confession.

'Sue, I don't know…' As my voice trails away I know there's something else I want to say about good and evil but the idea won't form itself into words yet.

'I don't.' Sue's voice is flat.

I feel the rough stone of the harbour wall digging into my calves as I turn my head toward her. She's sitting in the chair but I'm afraid if I touch her, she won't be there. Her face, so dear and familiar, is lost now with new grooves grown into sallow, yellowing skin. Her eyes have shutters over them. Sue, the only one of three daughters who has continued to be a practising Roman Catholic, who is bringing up her two sons in the faith, who has sent them to a Roman Catholic School, does not believe in God. Where can we go from here?

She is lost. I am lost. The gold of the sun is fading, but still the sea intensifies its rays before they spring back to surround us in an intimate circle of light. But we are at the dark and silent heart of this brilliance. The screeches of herring gulls, trawling for dead fish and quarrelling over discarded crisps and cheese sandwiches tossed aside by day-trippers, echo in my head. The fishermen shout instructions before setting off for their evening catch. These have been part of my scene, but now I hear them from afar as if in a dream. The contrast between the now of Sue's unbelief and the then of her certainty is chilling. I've wandered from one land to inhabit another without noticing the how or why of it. What can I say that will be of any use whatsoever? This is no theoretical discussion with the purpose of scoring debating points. It's about what you know inside of you. What you have faith in. What your rock is. Sue has leant against her rock and found it missing. I don't know how to help her.

I wait for any remembrances of our childhood that might be dredged up into the light and begin a conversation with her in my head.

'Sue, remember all those years ago when we used to go back and fore to Sunday school and catechism class on Saturday mornings?' I pause. Where am I going with this? 'The nuns in their black and white habits with their shiny wimples creased beneath their double chins. Did you ever wonder who they were?'

'Sister Agatha. Oh yes. If your eyes drifted for one moment, she'd pin you to the back of the pew with one of those questions you had no hope of answering.'

I allow my body to sink into the aching boredom of the long hours I spent sitting on hard wooden pews, kneeling on places unknown to cushions, until the knobbly bones of my knees bored through to meet the floorboards below. This time seemed to last for the whole of my life then. Why does my stomach revolve and sink when I remember the smell of the inside of the church, dusty and dim as the interior of an ancient tomb?

'They said God's love and forgiveness lived inside that church if you looked. But I never found it.' How can I be admitting this now, as I write? I don't remember thinking it at the time. What other outworn beliefs are locked in the mausoleum? The smell of incense grows behind my nose, as I remember the hours I spent trying to discover where it came from. Yes this was the time when I believed it appeared by magic. How long was it before I knew that Sister Agatha couldn't possibly know about the magic and so there must be none. It was all a gigantic hoax.

'It's strange, she was a woman – but when I think of her now she seemed to have shed everything that was womanly.' I feel my body close up and hug myself as I dare to let her face swim before me. Bloodless skin, tissue paper thin; small, pebble grey eyes sunk into deep sockets surrounded by washed-out pink rimmed spectacles; her essence carved from granite, sharp at the edges and unyielding at her centre. But more than that, there was something almost malevolent about her.

'Sue, do you remember that boy Robert I was at school with? A bus knocked him down. His legs were badly injured. Sister Agatha said it was the sort of thing that happened to you if you were not paying attention, if you weren't being good.' I shudder as the child's memory of that time is retrieved. 'That's when I gave up believing there could be a God, because I didn't want to believe there was such an almighty punishing being.' This is what I've forgotten, what I haven't wanted to remember.

♫

The sound of the harbour water as it ebbs and flows through my body rocks me with its comfort. I stretch out to hold Sue's hand as she speaks.

'The trouble is, I've waited until now to know the kind of God you came to know all those years ago. Somewhere inside me believes that is who God is. Someone waiting to catch me out if I slip my guard for one moment. And I have slipped my guard.' Sue struggles to allow more words to escape from her mouth. 'The treatment isn't working any longer. I'm going to die.' This knowledge has stretched between us, unspoken, for weeks, like the web spun by the spider, unseen until it appears in all its intricacy and beauty in the brilliant sunlight.

'Are you afraid?' What a stupid question I think. Of course she is. So am I.

'Yes I am.' Her mouth closes into a tight line. 'I'm afraid for me and for everybody. I can't do anything to stop feeling afraid. I feel so useless. I can't bear to leave Mike, the boys. What will happen to them? What have I done for this to happen to me?'

♫

I can't write any more of this at the moment. I have touched Sue's despair and, if I had recognised it then, my own. But I wanted to take her fear away; to be able to say something that would make it all right; would comfort her. But I couldn't. I had no idea what to say. What to offer. Now, seventeen years later, I think, *What if we'd gone into a church like the one at Chemayo in Colorado I went into last year? Would that have helped?* Before I visited it, a friend had told me it was a healing place. I don't know quite what I expected but certainly not what it was. But, as I left the crypt of the church, the memory of my mother visiting Lourdes some years before she died came back to me. She had returned full of her experiences. I couldn't understand then how they had renewed her. But at Chemayo, I realised that my mother hadn't gone to Lourdes looking for a cure, but had gone to strengthen her faith, which helped her to bear her suffering. In some indefinable way I sense now, as I write, that I have been held by guilt at not having been able to follow her way. This, another block to finding my own spiritual path, is beginning to dissolve.

There was a church on the harbour near where Sue and I were sitting. I resume the conversation, with Sue, in my head.

♫

Could we have gone into it? What do you think, Sue?

She turns her chair towards the harbour church. 'Come on let's go in. Give it one last try. Think you can stand it? It's strange. Taking communion still gives me some comfort.'

'I haven't been in one since… Well I can't remember when.' I jump up and push.

Flames of hundreds of candles light a dim crypt. Air is filled with curling strands of smoke and the smell of wax mixed with the cloying heaviness of incense. Crutches and callipers hang from blackened wood beams occupying every cranny of cramped space. Hand-written notes cover soot-encrusted, stone walls offering prayers. They ask for healing for a beloved daughter or son, husband or wife, mother or father, friend. Faded posies of flowers lie on flagstones. I watch a motionless Sue absorb the scene as it processes before us. A bell tolls for Mass and she motions for me to heave open the heavy oak door into the church. The priest enters, taking his place at the altar, white and gold vestments gleaming in shafts of light piercing through dusty windows into the shadowy interior.

His burgundy baritone sings, 'Kyrie eleison: Christe eleison: Kyrie eleison.'

As his voice sounds these words, they are filled with his feeling for them and their meaning and I feel I am hearing them for the first time. This is a far cry from the endless, rotelike services I remember from childhood.

At the end of the mass, we in the congregation, offer the sign and words of peace to each other. I turn to Sue. Her face is relaxed; the months of pain seeming to retreat as the weary paths etched across her face soften. Her wasting body lifts and straightens from within until she is settled on her chair rather than within it.

My heart takes me back to a time a few months before Sue died. She was waking from her afternoon nap and the room was heavy with summer heat. As she lay on her bed drawing herself up from the depths of sleep, her eyes opened and I saw that she was in what I could only describe as a state of bliss. How I knew what it was I don't know. She told me that a radiant angel of light had been hovering over her as she slept.

Now, in the church on the harbour, women, men, children are greeting each other. Sue opens her eyes. They sparkle with some new knowledge. The shutters have disappeared. She takes my hands in hers. 'Peace be with you.'

'Peace be with you, Sue.'

For one moment I'm filled with envy, for my sister knows something I don't. She is opening secrets it'll take me a long time to know.

Chapter Seven

Mary's Arrival

Chapter Seven

Mary's Arrival

On my return from Africa, I was captivated by images from the trip, some surfacing again and again in my mind often accompanied by feelings of sadness. I began to realise that these images of wilderness, desolation and family had in some way something to do with how I felt about my own life. I had a sense that the way in which I had lived it for so many years was of little interest to me and felt a waste of time. It hadn't been about all of me. There were still parts of me, which I knew I was not touching. I was beginning to understand how I had banished any spiritual dimension to my life, way back in my childhood. "Opening Secrets" emerged from a place of not knowing consciously, via the images brought back from Africa. I was also beginning to recognise how powerful a tool creative writing was. The soul's memories and yearnings could be revealed through mixing autobiography with "fiction". It could bypass my literal mind, to allow the unsaid and unacknowledged to emerge, often through poetic images, to speak far more clearly of feeling than the intellect. A fresh pathway had been opened up. It was to take me into the part of the jungle where all sorts of beliefs, rooted in what I had learned about myself as a result of my Roman Catholic upbringing, lurked. I set about the task of disinterring them.

At a regular meeting of our group, working with the Native American Medicine Wheel, I met with the spirits of six aspects of myself. The young teenager led me into her deep disquiet about showing herself. I needed her to speak to me.

In the Women's Group during this time, we were working with the stories of the Clan Mothers as told by Jamie Sams in her book *The 13 Original Clan Mothers*: *Your Sacred Path To Discovering The Gifts, Talents And Abilities Of The Feminine Through The Ancient Teachings Of The Sisterhood.*' At the monthly meetings of the Group, around the time of each New Moon, we meditated upon the stories of that month's Clan Mother, seeking ways of bringing her teachings into our everyday lives. We played games, meditated, drew pictures, painted stones, sang and chanted, drummed, danced, spent time in nature, and shared, or not, our stories of experiences, challenges, setbacks and successes.

As the year drew to a close, I went to Switzerland to spend Christmas with my nephew, Rich, my sister Sue's elder son, and on the flight back I saw a full circle rainbow reflected on the ground below.

This heralded a period of months when rage and despair alternated, as The Goddess Mary Magdalen presented herself and her hidden teachings. I was drawn ever deeper into my physical body through the summer, when I spent time at 'The Council of All Beings' at Magdalen Farm and later, on the island of Cephallonia, singing and moving.

The Communion Egg

I meditate.

I'm at a Council meeting of my Spirits. I've called to me my baby, young child, teenager, adult, wise one and incoming spirit. What have you to show me, I ask, about my present situation as I sit in the West on the Medicine Wheel, the place deep within? I'm shown a banana skin. The woman of wisdom tells me it's my mind, which will do its best to trip me up whenever it can. Mind again! My little girl tap-dances around the outside of the spinning wheel at great speed; she sings at the top of her voice. My graceful woman reclines on the wheel as it propels her round and round at a leisurely pace as the breeze ruffles her white dress. At the centre of the wheel my baby lies secure and untroubled. I can't see my teenager, though I had called to her to join us. This scene in a playground flickers before me until it's time to say farewell. My teenager appears; she has her back turned towards me. She will not acknowledge me.

♫

A friend gives me a healing massage one evening, at her home. She places some ointment on my brow. Its perfume sinks into the centre of my forehead, the brow chakra. The memory of an older fragrance fills my nostrils. It's the smell of the chrism, olive oil and balsam, used when I was confirmed as a Roman Catholic. I've forgotten all about it. This is a "Claudia" experience. Having left her cradled in the arms of the silver birch, with the Mistle Thrush singing to her, she's ready to reveal some more of her secrets. It seems she must trust me a little more now.

I'm eleven. Trying to remember the rules for being a good Catholic. The bishop is going to ask me about them before he anoints me. They don't make sense. So how can I remember the right answer for each question? I'm going to learn them parrot fashion.

'You're going to be made a full member of the Roman Catholic Church,' the nuns say.

I feel like a nun. To make up for my sins. I came into the world as a sin. It's like living in a convent. It's not safe to show myself in the world. How long do I have to make up for being a girl?

My mother used to say, 'once a Catholic, always a Catholic.'

I know I'm held still in the vice-like arms of "the faith." Even though I think I'm no longer a Catholic, somewhere inside me I'm caught in a web of spoken and unspoken beliefs and attitudes lodged at an age when I didn't understand them and certainly wasn't aware of their meaning. I'm beginning to notice the seeds of my resistance to things spiritual as they appear from different directions. Working in a shamanic way has uncovered my knee jerk reactions whenever anything comes up which reminds me of my early religious experiences. My dislike of the altar when I've been on the Red Road courses. My distaste, deepening into disgust, when I see other people genuflecting before it. The mention of prayer brings an image of a stone inside me. I say to myself I'll pray, but I don't believe it will make any difference. Part of me wants to touch something spiritual but another part resists. And what are Great Spirit and Great Mystery all about? It's said the Source is whatever you think it is, God, Allah, Love. So what do I think it is? I don't know and I feel I don't want to know. No that's not true. But when I do pray, I hear this voice inside me, it must be "Claudia's", saying *there's no point, because I know there's no one to hear. Nobody ever heard me when I prayed.* How do you know that? *I just do*, is her answer. I don't want to hold on to any of these beliefs any longer. Wrapped tightly within them is my deep, deep fear of death. I have to rewrite this fiction of "Claudia's" spirituality so that the grip of the Roman Catholic Church on me does not become terminal. It has poisoned the teenager and the adult.

I don't believe there is a God. But I've written into that belief and I've discovered the child, "Claudia", who made it up to protect herself from what she really knew. There is a God and he's not a pleasant being. He sits in judgement, just waiting for her to show who she really is. A sinner. This is what she learns in the years trooping back and fore to church. *I listen to the priest and nuns. They tell me what I've got to do so I'm ready to make my first communion. I'm seven.* She doesn't remember the service, though there's a communion breakfast in the priest's house afterwards. They have boiled eggs. She remembers them because they're a luxury in the 1950s. But communion's not the problem. *It's what I have to do to get there: go to confession. I'm wondering what I'm going to say this week about sins? There have to be some, every time.* The priest expects them, just as she knows there'll be a penance of some "Our Fathers" and a few "Hail Marys". *I can't think of any sins I've done. I've tried to be ever so good.* There's a space where sins are supposed to be. It's no good asking her. But I can hear her thinking. *I have to make some up. I quarrelled with my sister. That's sort of OK. I disobeyed my mum. She was quiet.* She has a catalogue of them because going to confession once a week on Saturday before catechism class is a must in preparation for receiving Holy Communion on Sunday morning. But her real sin is her secret rage at her Mum and Dad. It's so enormous that it cannot be allowed into the world. Left to fester, it obliterates any love she knows for them. This she can't confess because such feelings are unheard of; they're not listed in the catechism as possible sins. So, no confession means no absolution. She is damned. It's better not to believe, not to have "the faith". Then she needn't be burdened any longer with the weight of guilt her sin brings her. Her badness is interred in the deepest ground within her body. The next bit of fiction she creates is "There is no God". Now she won't have to face being consigned to the eternal fires of damnation. That's how she gets around her problem. She believes, with all her heart, that there must be no God anywhere.

Mary Magdalen

**Sometimes we need
to take a wider
view, to re-arrange
the margins of our
sight, let go the iron
tightness that
diminishes the
Light.**

Kay Leverton

As the plane lifts off the runway I watch the buildings of Basel dwindle into dolls' houses. The reflection of a complete rainbow appears on the ground. In my excitement I hit my nose on the window as I try to get a clearer look. It's the whirling full circle rainbow, the Sun Dog. I babble to my next door neighbour who has no idea what I'm talking about, but is impressed with my enthusiasm. Ten days ago, as I sat in a Sweat Lodge praying to know my way forward and find my dream, I asked for a sign to help me discover how I could achieve this. It's arrived today. In Native American teachings the Whirling Rainbow promises peace among all nations and all people. But I still have to confront more parts of myself, which I no longer need. They stand in the way of the harmony I seek.

♫

I return home and the memory of this moment dims. A shadowy figure of silent voice and unseen face hounds me over the following months. It resists with might my efforts to move forward with writing my book. I sit in front of the word processor and berate myself. This is what I've wanted to do for years and now the time and opportunity are here. But I meet an immovable block. I write into it. "Claudia" appears. I ask her to tell me more of her story.

She shows me the worn red cover of an exercise book and opens the pages.

It's my secret notebook. It's got stories of dreams I have on the top deck of the bus going home from school. I'm in my best seat right up front. Just window between me and the outside world. I sway along with the bus. It swipes the trees' branches hanging in its way. They part. I'm on a great white ship. It rushes through the seas to foreign lands. Africa is this day's stop. Palm trees wave their long green leaves over white beaches filled with big turtles. I fly over red and gold deserts and I'm looking down on zebra and antelope racing across plains. They swim swollen rivers watched by cunning crocodiles.

Cut.

It's another day. I'm like Margot Fonteyn, the world famous ballerina. I get standing cheers under the Arc de Triomphe in Paris. I'm dancing Odette and Odile in Swan Lake. In my white and black starched tutus I do twice as many fouettés as anybody else.

Cut.

The next day. I'm the greatest-ever-sportswoman holding high the Rose Bowl after winning Wimbledon with a miracle ace. And now I break the tape after running faster than any woman ever has to win an Olympic gold medal.

Cut.

Tonight I'm singing my heart out and Mimi dies of consumption in her Rodolpho's arms. He is lost without her. I cry.

I don't tell anybody about my dreams, but I visit them every day on my way home from school. Nobody's interested anyway; they've never asked. Then I just forget about them.

Why is that, "Claudia"?

Well, I always wonder if my Mum will be there when I get home. What do I do if she isn't? Where has she gone? Will she come back? I don't know why I think these things. She is always there. But she doesn't get up in the mornings any more before I go to school. I know something's wrong. She just says she's tired. My Dad gets breakfast and sees me off. I wonder what's wrong with her. Maybe she's ill. Perhaps she's dying. Have I done this to her? I don't tell anyone. They'll say 'Don't be silly, don't be stupid.' They don't understand anything. You can't believe what grown-ups tell you. They're not to be trusted. I listen to all the rules. Don't grumble or moan. Don't be unhappy, make a noise or show off. Don't put yourself forward and don't sulk. I work very hard at it. I must be very stupid if I have to learn to do all these things to be a proper person.

She decides.

I'm going to be like my Dad. He's never involved in all this. He doesn't have to confess sins. He doesn't have periods. He doesn't stay at home or do boring things all day. He doesn't nag and criticise. He doesn't say I have to be looked after all the time. He doesn't stifle the life out of me. He knows I've got what it takes in my head. He goes to work every day. That's where I want to go; to learn things, find out how the world's meant to be. Where you know what's right, what's wrong. A place where people aren't unkind and I can tell them what to do; where I can learn things from books and find the right answers. Nobody bothers with things like periods and being unhappy. They don't have time. I needn't be miserable when I live in my head. There are rules that everybody else knows about. I can learn them. There's a world where nobody gets silent and angry; where nobody's afraid; where there are no cats to love, just books and more books and exams and pieces of paper to say I've passed them. I'll do my duty and get it all right. I'll make sure nothing is known of what lives inside me. I am in charge.

I have forgotten to remember all this. What else have I forgotten?

♫

"Claudia's" in the darkened confessional.

The priest intones, 'For your penance say two "Our Fathers" and three "Hail Marys".'

I can see her fingering the sticky red beads of her rosary and silently mouthing, "Hail Mary full of grace! The Lord is with thee; blessed art though amongst women, and blessed be the fruit of thy womb Jesus. Holy Mary Mother of God pray for us sinners, now and at the hour of our death." The words join together in a chant whose meaning has vanished. It is a chore. "Claudia" sees the chipped plaster statue standing in front of her. A blue cloak covers the head, drapes across the folds of white dress. Mary gazes down upon her, Virgin and Mother. But she can't be both. It doesn't make sense. They say some statues of her cry, real tears. "Claudia's" never seen this one weep, so she can't be a sinner. Next to the Virgin Mary, Mary Magdalen, the prostitute, forgiven by Jesus for her sins, kneels. She's a sinner like "Claudia" and she's never been forgiven.

♫

I feel "Claudia" is signalling something important. So, I get down to some research at home. In the gospels, the Mary's are far more numerous than I realised. Mary of Bethany sits at Christ's feet in the house of Lazarus. Her sister Martha hurries around preparing the food and grumbling about Mary not helping. *I wanted to read Luke's account of this event at my sister, Sue's funeral, but the priest wouldn't allow it. The gospel reading was his prerogative. I still don't know why I chose that extract.* Then there's the sinful woman of Bethany, who washes Christ's feet and anoints them with oil. She could be Mary Magdalen, so could the woman who brings an alabaster casket of precious oil and anoints Jesus. Even the activist sister of Martha could be. And Mary Magdalen is healed of seven devils. She's present also at the crucifixion and alone, sees the risen Christ. But there's no mention in any of the gospels of Mary Magdalen, or any other Mary, being a whore. But that's how she's known. She's described as one of the women followers of Christ "out of whom went seven devils," when he healed her.

There are all sorts of differences in the gospel accounts. None of the scribes were there at the time of Christ, some weren't even alive at the time and what's more, all were men. It wasn't until three hundred years later that the Church Councils, consisting only of men, decided which gospels or parts of them would be in the bible.

♫

Several weeks pass while my findings buzz around inside me until I decide to meditate again in the hope of distracting my mind. Maybe some insights will emerge. One evening I settle by the light of a candle and wait.

♫

Going within, I find my resting self, wrapped in swaddling clothes. I sing a lullaby of breaths. In. Pause. Out. Pause. I watch inspiration snaking through the silver waters to rest in the stillness of the loughs and fjords of my body. Again and again the line of breath is spun, the song travels and now it tunnels its music into bone, muscle and cavity where cells wake, uncurl, expand, and spiral into life.

I sit. I wait. Silence grows in spaces between breaths. It brings the first snapshot of surrounding landscape. How it comes, what causes it, what coalitions there are between then and now, I don't know. Stillness is weighted down, full of heavy brown earth packed densely beneath, above, around, within me. Lightness and activity disappear. No sound disturbs the surface of thick mud until it begins to ooze in this sunless world. Dare I venture into a wasteland filled to brim with no hope? My body sags the distance between head and foot, crumpling as a sack of potatoes does in the emptying of it. I won't stay here any longer. It has nothing to tell me, nothing to show me that I want to hear or see. I've better things to do with my time. A story to write, a song to sing, friends to meet, food to eat. There is much I can fill my time with. But, here is where my song lives. Leaden weights hold me in place, waiting for moments to pass, just as dense coverings of cloud are blown on their way by strong westerlies, restoring clarity found at northern lights in night sky of indigo.

A scene in sepia, full of no image save for the rogue ramblings of mind's ceaseless chatter about this and that, processes before me. Let it go. But no, tenacious thoughts re-present themselves. There's been no resolution. Just the fading away of something precious but unacknowledged into a deafening silence, filled with unsaid words I hear now in my head. Will my mouth remain fixed, as though to cut off forever the words that could give shape to my feelings — too loud, too fierce, too demanding, too passionate to dare exposure? Must they remain loitering in the shadows of a dusty basement, missing yet another opportunity to join the light of daily life?

A roar seethes through this underworld. Molten lava spews resentments layered between slabs of isolation laid down through the ages.

Why, God, have you excised us women from your life, with the precision of a scalpel in the hands of a demented surgeon? You have consigned us to centuries of extinction? I can't scale the walls of your fortress lest I be slain by the sheer force of the arrows you send to repel me.

You sent your son Jesus here, but no daughter, to ensure that woman was honoured. Why did you leave it to all those male disciples to peddle their rubbish about women? Couldn't you have ensured the feminine voice didn't wither? You allowed it to be cloaked in shame and sin by the despots of the Roman Church. They created the fable of women who were either virgins or prostitutes. It lives today. If you are so powerful, how come you allowed that to happen? I thought you were omnipotent. Well your power is seriously dented. Can you hear the warped message that has been passed down the centuries? And why did you, Mary Magdalen and you, the Virgin, allow such misrepresentations to be propagated. God, did you have no faith in women? Who are you to send a son to earth and not allow his message to be heard through the ages? What do you really think about women? Why did you let your son come here and then fail to have the truth heard? Why did you send a son and not a daughter? Do you have a daughter? You must. Why haven't you asked her to be heard? How could you allow the men to hawk such trash? How do you expect a woman here to believe she is of you if you couldn't take the trouble to give her a voice? You let a group of men, who said they talked your truth, speak for you and your son, but not for your daughter. Why women, do we allow it to continue? Why don't we make our voices heard? Why don't I?

Heat seeping into the bones of my body since the earliest of all daybreaks is tired, and the cave of the longest day approaches. Sun is ready to set. Air has absorbed as much red dust it can bear. Now it weighs heavily on my eyelids, closing them without thought. Secret agent imagination operating in deepest silence orchestrates soloists and choir on wing. Blackbird tunes a tired ragged chorus, coughing and spluttering into the day's last song, each note placed with the utmost of care and abandon, like rare jewels cast into a womb of jet. The leaves of the tree under which I sit clap their hands in the newly arrived breeze until a rumbustious gust catches them in a wild ovation, tumbling the rays of sun pushing behind my eye in a dazzling display of coloured light.

The ear and eye of my heart wait, watch, listen. Jacaranda blooms, unhanded from their branches, float precisely to rest on the dry rusty earth below, settling around my feet into a deep pile carpet of rarest violet.

Silence deafens.

The moment comes.

I'm free at last.

I float among the branches of a baobab tree.

My body. It sits erect, cross-legged on the ground.

I can touch it. I can't feel it.

It's here. Yet I'm there.

A distant drumbeat echoes down the ages. It calls a return to Mother Earth. Each pulse reverberates in air spun since ancient times. I journey with them. Through desolate scrub made treeless by multitudes of elephants trekking to slake their thirst. In ghostly forests submerged by grey waters, trees stand naked of shade for beast or man. In gorges bereft of their power while streams wind idly over smooth boulders. Over nude mountains made purple by rays of sun, I come to rest on naked, crimson earth trodden from the beginning of Bushman time.

Here, where the ancestors' bones lie, I wait for stillness to return me home.

She speaks

My mirror is cracked by thousands of years of legend. Do not be bewitched by the words of the inaccurate reporters who down the ages have clothed the feminine in their ignorance and fear. Come to know their unknowing, for it is yours. Draw near to my experiences and hear the music, major and minor, of the words shrouding my mystery. I am a woman cursed for my sexuality and stripped of my femininity by the men of temples and churches. Forced to beg forgiveness for my truest nature, I know intimately the madness following this loss. Sink through swirling mire left by false fables. With the sights and sounds of hearted love, witness desolation, not turning aside or hiding behind your hands. With loving care and trust, wail at the death of each one of the truths of fiction. Colour the browns and blacks with the seven hues of the rainbow. And, when day dawns grey and sun sounds stone, see beyond appearances into the sacred space, the grail of the womb wherein lie your visions. Weave the dream, celebrating, creating, singing, writing, moving, melting into stillness. Then you, the inheritor of your divine light, will come to know your soul's spirit, the keeper of your loving passion, your reason for being here.

These images and insights swirl around inside me for weeks. I feel overwhelmed by the emerging task. What is the feminine I keep asking myself? It feels as though its meaning disappeared a long time ago. I return to more research, this time reading about the myths of ancient goddesses and some of the books that have been written about Mary Magdalen. They speak of the sacred feminine whose true meaning has become lost, written out of history. Instead, false fables have fossilised in the psyches of men and women. This is no longer just a journey through my own personal history. I am seeking something, which has not been honoured for thousands of years. I read of the "Sacred Women", priestesses of the Temple of the Goddess since 7,000 BC. This is a time when God is honoured and cherished as feminine throughout the Middle East and Europe. Such a woman would carry, in an alabaster bowl, the spikenard of a royal bride ready to anoint her sacred king. But she is divorced from her sacred role and suffers the madness of such a loss. Christ's healing of her seven chakras makes her whole once again. The feminine takes its rightful place in partnership with the masculine, only to be outlawed by the pedants and misogynists. But Mary Magdalen is present at the crucifixion, is the principal witness of the resurrection into everlasting life in spirit. Through embodiment in the flesh here on earth, we can come to experience spirit. As the seer, the visionary, the task falls to her of revealing the feminine. And, through it, the masculine, invisible to the mind alone, can appear.

I feel the heavy weight of thousands of years of the disbelief in the feminine blocking my way forward into my dreams.

Earthworm

I can move boulders.

Across the yard of Magdalen Farm, through an open gate I enter a field of bronzing corn. A rutted path follows hedge filled with hawthorn, bramble, nettle. It's Summer Solstice, a day loaded with blooming heat. Lethargy steals through my limbs and I sink to the ground, settling my back against the rough trunk of an aged oak; to wait for whatever will come with messages of healing and growth. My gaze idles around to where the land falls into a shallow bowl, before rising as a blue hill. Three trees stand on that horizon, rooted in the earth. Through narrowed eyes I watch them in the hazy distance. Separated by yards of turf from the remainder of their wooded family, they haphazardly straddle the top of the slope. This trio begins its dance to music unheard by me but seen in their stately progress. Mother, father, child of unknown origin unroll their minuet. Spreading, weaving, anchoring, approaching, retreating, trunk wraps around trunk, limbs twine, threading through bent branches. Leaves loll and sway from twigs. Roots writhe and twist, digging deep into stony earth. Across a bridge springing from my eyes, the body of my thoughts leaves me to sway across its span. At the eyehole where the base of the largest trunk opens, I enter its concealed passage on mouse's four legs, ears pricked, nose twitching. A triangle of dim sky, way above me, calls. Industrious ants march in procession to cart barrowfuls of crisp leaves, a morsel at a time, to feed their ravenous queen. Up and around I spiral through the musty interior until I burst through into the blue.

Crow, Keeper of Sacred Law is waiting. What have I to say for myself, she wants to know? I power a sound from my centre. It explodes and reverberates across the valley to where I sit. *Is this the creature I've been waiting for? Maybe yes, but maybe no. Oh you creatures do like to be mysterious!* She caws loudly, orchestrating images shedding light into shadows. Gifts stream from the dreaming cave of the West to become visible as the visions of the East. And in my field is someone who can assist me with the challenge of letting go of what hampers me in making this journey; for what is hidden is unnecessary and harmful to my survival. Crow leaves to continue patrolling the void.

I move on from the shade of the oak, drawn to lie down on a bed of grass under an overhanging willow. Light dapples my face. I close my eyes. *Who else will come? Some African beast, a zebra, an elephant or maybe a leopard?* Something's digging into my back. I squirm around and settle myself again. *Well, where are you? Whoever you are, I'm waiting.* Feathered grasses brush over my cheek. A bee swooping by my ear fills my head with its hum. I open my eyes; its rounded body feeds busily from buttercups. I loosen the elastic of my muscles and sink deeper into the earth, wriggling my back over the ridges of dried mud.

I drift on a breeze. *Something's trying to attract my attention. It's an earthworm. This isn't the glamorous creature I expect. I'll wait for something else.* The early afternoon bird chorus in the distance chats and sings half-heartedly. It's not time for the full-blown choir to get underway. *It's here again. I don't want it. I'm waiting for something more appropriate.* I compose myself. But it's here precisely because it's not what I'm expecting. It's not going away. Crow caws stridently from the oak at the corner of the field. *Yes I hear you; this must be the creature you were talking about earlier.*

The ravine reopens. Pale light shines into deep fissures gouged through its sides. Beyond, lies darkness into which earthworm plunges and I watch as her sightless dance senses my earthen world. Soft, slender, boneless, legless, no un-yielding shell protects her body. Stretching thin she wriggles through softened particles ploughing new tunnels. Absent ears allow no sound to disturb her. No smell tells her where she is, for nose is missing. Oxygen pumps through skin powering muscles. In heavy clay she makes space, shifting boulders fifty times her weight, casting aside swallowed soil, rich and ready to feed new growth. She surfaces with the onset of night to shift her shape into skin-shedding snake, the creator of new life from old. Her message tells me that yet more lies in the ravine, which I must raise to the light. This is a task of the deep where the true gifts of Mary Magdalen can be received.

The Cicada Blues

Heated gusts of air whip tablecloths across dishes of glistening purple stuffed aubergines and steamy green beans in tomato sauce. A gnarled tree loosens its unripe olives. A cat tears howling from the shelter of one table to another. The chair under me tilts on the crumbling concrete of the taverna floor. This is the island of Cephallonia where, fifty years ago, many buildings crumpled; destroyed by an earthquake.

'Did you feel that?' I ask one of my neighbours.

'What?'

'The ground tilted. D'you think it's an earthquake?'

'You've been reading *Captain Corelli's Mandolin*. It's just your imagination.'

'I don't think so.'

The Voice and Movement Group has transported itself almost en masse, for ten days moving and singing in an olive grove set on a hill beneath eagle-inhabited mountains and above blue Ionian seas. Our songs sung, our supper finished, we struggle through the black night up steep unlit roads, buffeted by wailing winds, serenaded by the bells of goats disturbed from their slumbers.

I wake from dreams filled with screeching, banging gales as pale gold creeps above the hill behind our apartments. One by one, the cicadas tune up for the day, as warming light spreads over their resting-places. The rattle of their orchestra spreads like a wild fire, unceasing in its labours until each night sun slips into sea.

Nine of us are staying in these newly completed apartments high above the village of Lordata. It's a thirty-minute trek down to the olive grove, overlooking the sea, where we sing. It's far too hot to return up the steep hills at lunchtime. So, after breakfast of yoghurt and fruit, we scramble around looking for towels, hats, sunscreen, mats, bikinis, swimsuits. Then it's down winding hills, past browning fields where the goats watch us rather haughtily from rocky outcrops.

'I've forgotten my torch,' I shout. It'll be pitch black before we return tonight.

'It's ok. I've got mine,' someone else shouts.

'Thanks.' That saves me struggling back now. It's not yet ten o'clock but the sun is intense. The island is in the midst of a heatwave and by midday the temperature will be in the mid to late thirties.

I move from shade to light, under heavy bougainvillaea laden with dust. Around one last bend, the sea disappears and the road straightens to drive through the village of Lourdata; two mini-markets, a few tavernas, one small boutique (where I've bought two sarongs), and a spring. We make a quick stop to buy bread and fillings and fruit for lunch and to fill our bottles with icy water from the mountains. Then we continue, downhill again, to the grove.

The harmonium drones 'Sa' as twisted trees provide shade from the strongest of the sun's rays. Black olives hang, slowly growing heavy with their oil. We move in the sun-sodden air on red earth covered with stony remains of hundreds of fallen olives. Our bodies loosen, as heat seeps through skin, into blood, bone and muscle, opening up spaces through which sound needs to travel. One by one, the voices announce their presence.

A 'Sa' from one is joined by another and yet another, all tuning up. A 'Ma' joins in, then a 'Re'. As they disappear, another 'Sa' sails on the breeze and a 'Pa' answers and then a 'Ni' questions. A 'Da' pushes higher. The improvised harmony weaves its way through the trees, challenged by the steady accompaniment of the cicadas.

I grow my voice. I round it. Is it pitched in just the right place? Too much control of skeleton, it shelters close. Too little, I could fall over. In the shade of two olive trees, a flute and a tampura join the harmonium. With our sounding, ten movers fill with the breath of oxygen, and bend, stretch, twist, shape and re-shape.

I return to the place inside me where I find "Claudia", whom I left with the birch tree in Surrey. She's devoted herself to burying memories deep in my body where they lie forgotten by my mind, interred in earth. As I improvise movement and sound with the orchestra, I ask "Claudia", *please release your memories. Let me be in the moment, living in my eyes, neck, legs, torso, arms, hands, feet and fingers; expressing my body's wishes without your fiercest instructions not to enter it.*

And so she raises the blinds shuttering me from the outside world and it from me. I make myself present to my inner space. Energy moves my limbs, threading, weaving, moulding a dance of my steps.

The thread freezes.

I wait, resting, lying, standing, while "Claudia" has her silent way. I hear no voice but her will prevails. She cannot support the intensity of my offering my conscious self.

As I watch my companions, a twined ball of sorrow, for places deserted so long ago, rises within me. It moves through my body, shaped into a desire flowing through my arms, hands, fingers. It says 'I am beautiful' over and over again. As my offering draws to an end I hear a litany in my head. *What do you think you've been doing? Showing yourself like this. Showing off. Showing who you are. You are not beauty. It is a vain wish.* These are the words, which stopper me up.

But here in Cephallonia I cast off that voice for now and dip to the earth caressing it's worn antique beauty.

At lunchtime the heat is in the early thirties. Down the road, across the sand, I fall into the embalming waters of the sea. Floating on my back, ripples washing over my stomach and breasts, I hear the notes of my *Cicada Blues* pulsing through my body. But they herald something else waiting to burst into my consciousness. It forms itself, as forest fires on neighbouring Zakynthos island belch bands of grey smoke to fill blue sky. As I struggle to move in my body and from it, I will go into the sea topless. The wound of my absent breast has been waiting to be heard. Why should I hide it? At dusk, as the sun melts into a globe, I sink naked into the sea, celebrating with my companions.

Chapter Eight

The Wounded Masculine

Chapter Eight

The Wounded Masculine

The arrival of the Goddess Mary Magdalen had helped me realise that how I felt about being a female had roots which stretched back thousands of years. I felt outrage at the extent of the conditioning and beliefs about the nature of women, which had been laid down through the ages; the sum total of which resided in me, just as it must in other women. My mind found it difficult to comprehend that at one time the feminine had been sacred and had played a leading role in determining the way in which the world and its communities were organised peacefully. I was just about overcome at the enormity of my task. I had asked what prevented me finding my dream and I was discovering there was plenty. I needed to move yet deeper into the imagination of the Goddess for more clues about my dream and what was still preventing me retrieving it.

In the months following my return from Cephallonia, I continued to discover the truth of what it meant to have the four bodies I had learned about during the healing and chakra workshops six years earlier. I was experiencing and gaining understanding through each of my mental, emotional, physical and spiritual bodies. The physical was the only one I could see but the others were becoming more real to me every day. The beliefs I had were many layered and faceted. Change crept through me bit by bit. Journeying around the Medicine Wheel showed me clearly that when painful memories were retrieved there was only so much of their pain that I was able to confront at a time. There were many, many learnings in so many different ways about suffering. When any problem appeared I was shown from each direction on the wheel, distinct and deeper aspects of it. I felt the tentacles of my beliefs, attitudes and behaviours were spread wide, deep and long. Patience was something I desired but often despaired of cultivating.

In December, at the time of the Winter Solstice, I returned to Magdalen Farm to attend a Sweat Lodge ceremony, led by Jack Angelo, in the North of the Medicine Wheel. In this place of Air and Mind I sought clarity and wisdom. I offered prayer and gratitude for all of my life's experiences. I wanted to shed yet more of the old but still strong beliefs that held me chained to a way of being that left me feeling stultified. I had attended such ceremonies a few times before but I was filled still with the usual dread at the prospect of heat, vapour and darkness accompanying the ceremony of prayer, purification and transformation.

A few days later I left to spend Christmas walking in Sicily with friends. It was there I experienced, for a moment, the arrival of the masculine light. This heralded a time of more disruption than usual over several months in the New Year. It was during this period that I recalled a trip I had made the previous autumn to Ireland to dig yet deeper into the Roman Catholic roots, which were my legacy. And the wounded masculine appeared.

Purifying Fire

The door closes on black sky heavy with sodden clouds. I am enclosed with eleven companions in the pitch-darkness of this circular Sweat Lodge. I lower myself to the ground and wriggle into a comfortable sitting position; hay, which we laid on the floor earlier, scratches my bare legs. We sit, scrunched up together, in a circle around the walls of the Lodge. Seven red-hot stones, which the Firekeeper passed in on his long-handled shovel before the door was closed, lie in a pit at the centre of our circle. Jack, who is leading the ceremony, pours water onto them. Clouds of steam laden with sage and cedar brush my cheeks, fill my nostrils, choke and gasp in my throat. Hot fumes move through tubes, my breath rasps in my lungs.

Sweat pours from my silted pores. Incense smokes through my brain's blocked channels sifting, airing, opening.

I sit in my imagination at the top of a mountain. Mustard haze glazes air filled with smoke belching from factory chimneys spread over sprawling plains. It shrouds a no longer verdant valley far below, where dun-coloured water glistens. A river loops back and fore, sluggish on its long trail to the sea. Wizened trees with greyed leaves thread through forests. Sulphurous murkiness meets clear blue sky overhead. Air, the territory of mind, is where my pollution lives.

I won't be able to take this heat and darkness for long. I'm going to suffocate. This is just the beginning. I've got to get through as much as an hour in this. *I can't do it. I'm next to the door, I can get out easily. If I do I'll be really envious of the others. I won't have done what I've come here to do. I'll have failed. Well I'll stay for this first round. See how it goes.* The person next to me is clinging to my arm. She wants to get out.

'Don't let me,' she whispers.

That does it, I can't go now.

I listen to the others as in turn they pray. *This is much better. Something else to think about. Encourage and support. Forget the heat and blackness. Funny, I'm getting used to them. I think I'll be able to stay.*

Finally, it's my turn. 'Great Spirit, hear my prayers. Help me to release the poisons holding my dream, prisoner in the cave of the West. I want to let go of all my childhood beliefs that God is a tyrant. I pray to know my Essence.' My cheeks are burning.

'I give thanks for all my experiences whether I think they're good or bad. For having had cancer; it's taught me so many lessons about my negative ways. I give thanks for my family and the lessons they show me. For writing, singing, friendship, wisdom, abundance. For the little soldiers who patrol my thoughts jeering and diminishing any of the talents I claim.'

I remember promotion at work. It held no real value only relief that I had not failed. Hadn't been found out. The words I wrote, the staff I managed, the negotiations I made. Anyone could do those things. But others, I discovered as I left work, valued them as uniquely mine; something different from what another person might give. What is pride in one's labours, I wonder? Is it one of the seven deadly sins or a way of caring for the soul? I want so to believe the latter, but the nagging voice has messages about showing off. Little girls are seen and not heard. I have a feeling that to care about my gifts and to feel pride in them is to prostitute myself. I've completed my prayers. The leader of the ceremony calls for the Firekeeper to open the door. I drink some water from a bowl we pass around and relax for the moment.

Until this morning, the plot on which we, the Lodge participants are sitting, has been a small space in a field, on Magdalen Farm. We come to it after a day of preparing ourselves, through the ritual and ceremony of sharing our stories, visioning, drumming, dancing, singing, chanting and making our prayers. We cut willow for the frame of the Lodge, and gouge a hollow where its centre will be. The Firekeeper and his assistants dig a pit outside to house the fire. We use the displaced turf to create an altar nearby and collect wood ready to feed the flames in which the stones will heat for many hours. Rain begins to fall as we stake strips of willow, the frame for the Lodge, into the ground and bend them into the shape of an upside-down bowl about four feet high. There won't be enough room to stand upright inside. The string person supplies pieces of twine, orange and blue, made sacred by use in previous ceremonies, to tie the frame into place. The farm's pet pig joins our workforce. With play on her mind, she circles and snuffles likely candidates for games of chase. Should anyone join her and then dare to leave, she charges their legs reminding us that life can be fun. The building of the Lodge is a serious task to be undertaken lightly. We place layers of blankets, some once fine tapestry curtains and lastly a black tarpaulin over the woody skeleton until no light can be seen from the inside. Outside we place rocks in the fire-pit, ready to be heated later in the day. A deluge sweeps across the field turning ground we have trodden into squelching mire.

It's time for another round of prayers. The Firekeeper brings seven more heated stones from his fire-pit outside. One last breath of chill air fills my lungs and he closes the door. Hotness and blackness intensify. I'm deep in the womb of Mother Earth. I'm the very young child, I once was. *I'm digging with one of mum's silver teaspoons in the back garden. Trying to get to Australia. I know I have to go through fires at the centre of the earth. I give up in disappointment many times. The earth never feels warm no matter how deep I make my hole.*

Suffocating steam rises to fill my over-saturated body. Every pore oozes escape, escape. *Let my turn to pray come quickly. I can't wait, don't hesitate. At last.* I pray for healing for all those with illnesses of the mind, trapped in a kaleidoscope of endless silent censure, no longer able to function.

We've completed all our prayers. I crawl out into the night giving thanks to Mother Earth, and place my prayer tie in the fire. I leave with my supporter, who has been waiting outside the Lodge. She has been sending her energy and prayers to me throughout the ceremony. My bare feet are sucked into oozing farm mud.

Two hours later I stand outside the Lodge across the field and to the north of the Firekeeper. Clouds scud around the washed moon. I'm outside the Lodge, supporting my partner with my prayers and energy as she participates in the second purification ceremony of the evening. The rain has ceased. Night is dank. Dim shapes are scattered around the pasture, intent on supporting their partners in the Lodge. The Firekeeper stokes the flames. The aura of the Lodge appears through my meandering gaze. A grey, speckled fuzz grows to envelop the black bowl in a filament of coral and magenta. I narrow my unfocussed eyes and empty my mind as, in the pit, flames wrap around once wet wood, soaking yet more stones in heat. Rows of grey headstones rise from the seat of the fire to stride through unknown cemeteries laid across rolling fields of poppies as far as my eye can see. These images collapse into the furnace to rise again as a bridge of terracotta, spanning the altar, before reaching the place where the lodge has now faded from sight. Snake rears from the heart of the blaze, hissing. It retreats as three cockerels stride across blackened stumps of wood, crowing loudly. From the conflagration, a Greek temple of shimmering white stone supported by towering columns emerges, filled with light. From behind me, Wolf makes her way towards the site of the lodge, circling the fire once before moving off into the darkness in the south. More than an hour has passed while these visions have set themselves into my psyche. I move forward to support my partner as she emerges through the door of the lodge.

Shed Some Light

She shimmers above me, her backdrop an azure sky as I climb through fresh, thick snow layering her lower slopes. My legs complain. The effort to lift their dead weight brings me to a complete halt. The energy of the past week has dwindled away. My throat is sore. My tickling nose explodes sneezes spluttering through crystal air. I thought I had been invited to visit her but I have been refused entry to the top of her flanks. The dormant poisons activated by the Sweat Lodge ceremony are surfacing through my body. I slump in crisp sunshine to wait for my companions' return from their ascent of the one with a yawning crater, Etna. As skiers and toboganners slide down the hillside in front of me, my thoughts drift back to the beginning, six days earlier, of this Christmas holiday in Sicily.

Giant hailstones greet us on 23rd December as our group of fifteen walkers leaves the hotel to trek into the hills. Our leader counts us out, just as he'll count us on in our return at the end of the day. But we are driven back, to wait until the stones cease their bombardment. Later, as we walk through the hills above Francavilla, the air carries sharp winds, and bouts of rain. Grey clouds envelop Etna. She appears now and then to glower from within her thick covering. The following day, Christmas Eve, she's clean, white, spouting fumes to feed the only shred of gauze in pristine blue. Golden sun knights her. Some day she will forge magic again from her flaming lava. A mud track leads us towards Mount Baldo. In the distance the crowing of a cockerel bites through the clear air. Trees, dressed in bottle green leaves, laden with oranges ready to drop, line our way. I imagine the red juice sliding over my tongue. A tarmac road winds our way around foothills in steep curves until we reach an abandoned village nestling at the head of the valley. This is no ancient ruined settlement but a collection of concrete shells: homes built for dispossessed Sicilians returning after the Second World War. This might have been a paradise. But everybody left. A small bare church stands in prime position looking straight down the vale to the sea. Chanticleer heralds our arrival and sunlight streams through a paneless window illuminating the ghostly shape of Christ on the wall above, where once, the altar stood.

We take to steep rocky paths carved by goats. I practice being nimble and surefooted, but I don't have four legs.

Through terraces created 2,000 years ago by Roman invaders, where once corn grew almost to the mountaintop, we reach the summit of Baldo. It lives up to the sound of its name. Bare bones, bleached, soaked and worn by centuries of rain, sun and wind are dotted with grey moss. Far below me, Taormina, pink buildings set crazily into sheer rocky faces, and a Greek theatre perched perilously on a cliff edge, stretches in hazy sunlight.

'The French call Taormina the St Tropez of Sicily,' one of our group tells us.

'Well, we'll find out when we get down there,' someone else says.

'I've never been to St Tropez. I wouldn't know the difference,' I say as I bite into an enormous crusty roll filled with pecorino cheese.

My neighbour sitting next to me on the mountainside says, 'There's a lot of up and down, and not much along, on this island.'

I ponder on this. 'No wonder most of the Sicilians are short and stocky. I don't know why but it seems to me that being short must be an advantage when walking the hills. Something about the centre of gravity. I suppose.'

'Maybe they've just become stunted – like the Welsh,' she jokes looking at me.

'I'm not stunted.'

'No. You're an exception to the rule.'

We're on the move again.

Descending to the coast, we follow swaying mule tracks skirting derelict buildings striving to remain standing in the middle of nowhere. A mountain farmhouse long deserted; roofs and windows absent; grey stone walls tumbled into heaps of rubble; a tree waiting to bear olives lurching horizontally across what once was a kitchen. The strident voice of the rooster calls for attention. *Yes, three cockerels appeared in the fire at the lodge. There's something about them signifying betrayal.* Further on, a stately villa of dull orange brick has its doors locked and barred while the collapsed tiled roof opens it to the elements. We reach a flight of one thousand worn steps laid down by the Greeks more than two thousand years ago. At their lower reaches, the Stations of the Cross carved in stone escort us into Taormina. A lone piper steps out along narrow cobbled streets as he blows a local lament on his goatskin bag. Wealthy Sicilian and Italian tourists, men in cashmere overcoats, women in long glossy fur coats, eye us walkers in our muddy trousers, boots and T-shirts. They snigger, not politely behind their hands, but openly. Ah, the British! We straighten up and march past, saluting as we go.

Back at the hotel, a seven-course Christmas Eve dinner awaits us.

'At least it'll be a change from turkey and sprouts,' someone jokes.

But in this home of pasta, turkey and sprouts nestle between spaghetti and chocolate torta. Later, we walk down into Francavilla and assemble in the square outside the cavernous church with a lot of the locals. Nearby, the bonfire blaze, lit several hours earlier, is fading. I don't know what I'm waiting for. I slide into the back of the church. Scarlet poinsettias surround a chanting priest clothed in white robes. The blooms tumble in rivers down the steps of the altar towards the rail separating the congregation huddled over their rosaries.

I creep out into the frosty night. At midnight, the huge wooden church doors open. Young and old pour into the night to greet waiting friends and families. Fireworks explode and bells chime until silence descends upon the crowd.

The priest enters in procession with the baby Jesus in his arms. As did the Pagans, long before the coming of Christ, he processes through the streets to show the people the coming of the light.

Tara's Presence

Home from Sicily and it's New Year's Eve. My sniffles are growing. At a party I'm invited to choose, sight unseen, a Rune. It's Hagal, the "hailstone"; it heralds a time of disruption. *So, the scene was set in Sicily.* My cold becomes a longer lasting virus. I cancel the new workshops I've planned, to introduce people to their healing voices. These are based on my own experiences of how voice and movement work have helped me to access buried emotions in a way that counselling alone has not. But I can barely speak, let alone sing. Confusion and disarray stalk through my life. *I thought I knew what*

I was meant to be doing? Where am I supposed to go from here? I'm totally off balance. It's time to review the events of the past few years. But where do I start? I sit, at home, in despondent silence while endless chatter exhausts itself.

Tara emerges.

My thoughts return me to a trip to Ireland, I made with a friend in November, a few weeks before the Sweat Lodge ceremony at the Winter Solstice. When we decided to make the journey, we were both unclear about what its focus should be. We each had ancestors from different parts of the country, mine were from near Skibberene in County Cork. But I felt the need to resolve something about this part of my heritage. We agreed to think about where we might go and get in touch shortly. A few days later, I came home after work to find a message on the answer phone from this friend.

'I think it's an excellent idea of yours to go to Newgrange. I've been reading about it. It's an ancient site. Like Stonehenge. Give me a ring.'

I rang her back. 'What's this about Newgrange? I've never heard of it and I didn't talk about it'

'Yes you did. Definitely.'

So, here we are at Newgrange! We've crossed on the ferry from Pembroke Dock to Rosslare and driven through counties Wexford and Wicklow, around Dublin into County Meath. Not far from Drogheda, we've come to an area known as Bru na Boinne, lying within a curve of the River Boyne. There are about forty ancient monuments here, one of which is Newgrange. It is a passage grave, older than the pyramids of Egypt. We're huddled together with about thirty other visitors in the central tomb chamber, marvelling at its construction. Only at sunrise on the shortest day of the year, direct sunlight enters this chamber, not through the doorway of the passage, but through a narrow slit under the passage roof at its outer end. Everywhere, the eternal spiral motif decorates the stones of the grave. *It's impressive but I don't feel moved by it.*

It's the following day when I do feel some great connection with the land of this area. We drive past fields greyed in pale November sunshine. Whipped clouds swirl across blue sky. We're searching for Tara. On the map it's not far away but the signposts seem to be sending us in a spiral.

It was my grandmother, my mother's mother who came from County Cork. Like all of my ancestors, she's bequeathed things to me, some of which I may no longer want. Or there could be other things I may want to reclaim. Whatever they are, this is time to reflect on her life, what little I know of it. Her baptismal name was Honora Neil, not Nora O'Neil as she had always claimed. This only came to light when, at the age of seventy, she needed a passport for the first time. A copy of her birth certificate arrived from the church in Ireland where she was baptised. She also discovered that she was a couple of years older than she claimed. I suppose there was nothing strange about that, for she was well known in the family for fiddling with time, forever putting the clocks in the house back because she knew that my grandfather always moved them forward. He liked to be early for everything. After my aunt, her eldest daughter died, just before I went to Colorado, I was sorting through her possessions and found the only photograph I had ever seen of Honora as a young woman. It must have been taken on her wedding day. I was startled to see my eyes looking out at me. When I knew her, I felt little if any connection with her.

What do I remember of her? A grey-haired imposing figure, tallish, with a large bosom. Well, often elegantly dressed, she wore lots of large sparkling rings sliding around her fingers. I have one of them now. In her hey day she was quite a golfer apparently, hence her nickname, Birdie. When I was a child, she used to make peppery bread sauce to accompany roast chicken. Both were expensive delicacies for me. It's hard to imagine now that chickens were a luxury in days before battery-reared hens came tumbling out of deep freezers.

I allow my child's memory of her to surface. *She drinks whisky and soda just like the men, not sherry like the other ladies. I'm afraid of her. I don't know why. I just am. She doesn't feel like a grandma. I know I don't really matter to her. She has her favourites and I'm not one of them.*

I did glean bits and pieces about my grandmother from my mother and my aunt, before they died. Honora didn't keep in touch with her family in Ireland once she left there after her marriage. She also had a vicious temper. When her daughters were young, they felt the full force of it at times.

I remember my mother saying, not long before she died, 'My Mum and Dad used to have violent arguments. When I was about four years old, I decided I was never ever going to get angry. It was too dangerous.'

Anger went underground. As a child I sensed it was there in my mother. And I am discovering it in me. The thread of rage joins three women, grandmother, mother and granddaughter. I see, yet again, that I am tangling with unresolved business.

At last we've reached Tara's high plateau. Her journey began in Tibet ten thousand years ago. As the Great Mother Earth, she spread through the world as Kuan Yin, Gaia, the Virgin Mary. In Ireland, where the River Boyne marks the boundary between two worlds, Tara has guarded the Seat of the High Kings from a time stretching back to before the Trojan Wars. I have business here with culminations. I'm not sure what they are, why they are important, but I embark upon a ritual designed to bring them into my consciousness. I stride across the green mantle of the Royal Enclosure. My feet sink into springing turf, the power firing from the earth beneath them takes my body where it will. An intricate pattern I cannot decipher is being woven. All the while I give thanks for the lessons I have been shown in the spiritual work I have done. For the gifts I have resurrected, which have lain fallow for the years of my lifetime – writing, singing, voicework, counselling. All these are to be honed into something more than I can comprehend for the moment. Nine times I circle the Bronze Age mound where worms consumed the bodies of hostages imprisoned by the ancient king, Cormac Mac Art. I pray for my way forward to be made clearer to me.

♫

From Tara we return to Rosslare to spend the night before catching the ferry back to Wales. In the early hours of the morning I wake up. I have been dreaming. My ancient wisdom is under attack from heavily armed and hostile forces, active for thousands of centuries. Shards of fear are lodged in my throat where my screams have been felled.

♫

Now, more than two months later, Tara has returned. I wonder why.

You prayed to me then. Now is the time to listen and watch.

As I sit with the Great Mother her spiral leads me to sift yet deeper into her body. One by one I call upon each of my roles to gather around her in circle.

The counsellor speaks. My skills grow as I witness others' courage as they unravel the stories their souls have to tell them. I sit with their trauma, offering through my compassionate heart, the safety they need, the comfort they deserve. Together we shine light to illuminate indistinct signposts pointing the way ahead.

The singer sings. Like the archaeologist, painstakingly I continue to uncover my ancestral voice buried deep within me. It speaks of times unremembered, and sings fragments of lost dreams I have still to unravel. I use these experiences to help others explore their voices.

The participant in the Women's Group walks her talk. I travel with my companions through the months and season's of the Thirteen Clan Mothers, exploring and celebrating the truths of the feminine. We show our mirrors to each other; reflections of immobility, hindrance, remembering, reclaiming, moving, grieving, growing. And now we part, giving thanks for the many gifts received and given, some noted, others unrecognised.

The writer picks up her pen. I hone my writing skills and draw together my journal, shaping it ready for the book I want to write. By the light of a candle in the darkness, writing liberates my words until their unknown power stoppers me up.

The traveller of paths abroad rests in the circle. I've visited other lands, Africa, America, Europe, my outer journey expanding the inner following the song lines on foreign territory.

I sit in the embrace of the Great Mother as I see each of these women, all aspects of me. But I do not feel their reflections in me. They are distant. I can touch them but not hold them. In my heart, the Great Mother shows me I cannot honour them, I cannot value them. What is missing?

♫

Over many weeks I have to allow my experiences in Ireland, the Sweat Lodge and Sicily to move through me. During this time my thoughts are sentinels. They stand motionless, holding captive the sleeping snake, rising from the flames of the Sweat Lodge fire. They scrutinise my actions, my feelings, and my intentions, reducing them to rubble. Like Peter, when the cock crowed three times, they betray my song when it speaks of the internal landscape, scrubbing it clear of the seven hues of the rainbow. I reach deeper into the temple of the feminine, this huge, seemingly bottomless bowl as it rests inside my body. I feel no passion for these women. I do not live in them. There is no fire filling them or me. Where is my love in all this?

♫

One evening, in exasperation, I sit at home by the light of a candle and meditate.

Tara, the Great Mother speaks.
'You continue to leave your heart to please others not just once but again and again. Your heart is where your home is, a place still not yet familiar to you. Within it lies your soul. It waits yet again to speak to you of events dark and light. The memories lie in your body. Let your tears fall and in the cauldron of their waters, be the fisher of your soul. Let them

lead you through the barren soil and desert sand to the cool oasis. The thunder beings speak of your raging fire lighting the way to the fears lying deep within your body. These fears, like the thicket, trap your heart, a bloom of rosiest pink now made pale by the weighty judgements of others you make yours. Water the desert soil so that the full bloom of the flower might appear where now there is barrenness.

Who speaks to you of duty? It is the duty of the martyr. Ask what you forego to meet another's needs; whose voice tempts you along a false path; who repeats the message of long ago that you are not worth nurturing. Duty speaks of false laws of reason and logic. The heart speaks of the way of loving and knowing; that is the path of the human. Do not flatten who you are to fit others' expectations of you.

Disease means no elbow room. Where are your elbows? Are they tied to your body or extended as a bird's wings in flight?

Do not make yourself and your efforts small in order to please, to leave undisturbed someone else. Make your kitchen your palace. Your soul grows in memory of the flavour of life on this earth. Your dishes evoke a memory of times simple, when the beast and the plant were happy to feed your growing life. The charm of the dream unfolds in a way to show you the links between the feeder and the fed.

Do not deny yourself in false modesty or place anyone or anything above or beneath you.

Do not allow yourself to be shamed, as you have been shamed.

Do not allow others to pluck your strings to make their lives happier. If you are not happy to have your strings plucked, then they cannot be happy to pluck your strings. The sound of their notes carries their own message if they care to hear, not yours.'

The Guerilla

As the season of spring approaches, I dream.

Death comes from two directions into the kitchen of my house in Africa. From the front, food poisoning quakes and streams through the door. I repulse it with my broom. I turn. Facing me is a black man. He has entered from the desert garden at the rear of my house. In his arms he cradles a machine gun and motions for me to sit at the table.

Yet more days are full to the brim with inky inertia, shrouding my thoughts, weighting my labours, flattening my spirit. I'm stranded in an isolated cell in the midst of the sightless and the silent. I cannot colour the events of my life, then or now, with meaning or purpose.

♫

One day, at home, I take a 'Sa' and wind my way through the scale of the wild melancholy Flamenco only to reach the iron bars of a prison. Spitting and snarling, a pacing leopard dares me to come further. A frenzied fandango of red and green lights fights to a standstill. I can no longer reach my song. The feral cat roars the way ahead with a primal scream starting in the deepest reaches. I wrap my voice into it, around it, through it as it winds and creaks from its tomb. Its screeching echoes in my red blood cells. 'Can't you hear me? Are you deaf or am I silent?' This great cat reverberates through the pit of my stomach, banging inside muscles, pushing ribs to their widest expanse. This is no quiet soldier staggering to his execution where a lethal dose will send him to the terrors of another world.

'Why do you consign me to this purgatory of "I've been meaning to contact you?" I'm waiting for a sign. Behind a thin veil, I watch you patter around. Washing, ironing, cooking, meeting, and speaking all those false words you think the truth, but are lies. You retreat into the rooms of your house saying, what is the matter, with the studied niceness of the quick-setting varnish of a homespun story that bears no resemblance to the truth. I cannot stay and face this quiet death inflicted every day in the pursuit of safety.'

♬

I take my brush and paint, shaping and colouring the man of this dream. Small, compact, he stands legs astride, clothed in a camouflage outfit of greens, browns and black. Hand grenades hang from a wide belt slung around his waist. He raises his massive gun, to rest across his shoulders and fires a red heart at a bat flying through blue sky. This is no man but a young boy. I sit him at my kitchen table and feed him with my sorrow for a long lost son. Spurned over and over again, he left, unwanted and unmourned, years ago. I weep well and deep at his banishment as I begin to hear his voice.

'I have gifts that are yours. But I armour my heart until the hurts inflicted upon me no longer touch me.'

He recedes into the shadows and the man he becomes speaks.

'I'm disgusted you write about these painful matters. Most people die before ever thinking about them. But you, you write about them. People will read the words you weave and say isn't it lucky I've never felt like that. These are weaknesses not to be borne. Yesterday no longer lives. There is only today and tomorrow. Be strong like me. I hear the call to war. I answer it, slaying enemies with thought, word, gun, shell. I am a fine brave person. I am powerful. I feel no dread, frenzy or mistrust. I know it is right to meet force with force. I am beyond question. I do it for my God, my country. It is always right to go to war. There's no banality, stupidity, ignorance, self-satisfaction, smugness in it. I do what I have to. Millions like me die at Passchendaele for their country. This is no blind and stupid world. I say sacrifice love for the power of the firing tank, mustard gas, repeating rifle. Crucifixion, genocide. Eliminate all who are different. Then we'll feel safe. Ignore, poke fun, criticise. These put pay to all other ambition. A good war solves all problems of the recalcitrant youth. It makes men of them. Answer my call. That's what we need. Bloody conflicts fed by the youth of the ages filing to earth to fill the trenches of Flanders with their broken bodies. They look for adventure. They find dismembered bodies twisted and torn, layered in this land of no man. Heads shatter. Trees explode. Craters blast into being where once the cow grazed and the potato flowered. Minds battered by the blast, blast, blast of bazookas live on in hell. I am the man of your nightmares who stalks you… until you slay me.'

The youth returns from the shadows.

'You blind liar. Standing, watching our bodies explode into pieces. You scramble minds until we can't remember how to speak. You bury us up to our necks in the bog land of war. We wait to die under burning sun or in frozen winds. Millions of us blown up through the ages. Can't you hear us groaning in silence? Listen to our hearts' quenched song lines.

I'm the man of your dreams.'

Chapter Nine

Storyteller

Chapter Nine

Storyteller

The disinterring of the feminine had led me into the masculine. We all contain these two major archetypal energies. The territory of the feminine is the soul, the inner life. Through feeling and sensation I had come to know more of who I was, rather than who I thought I was; who I had learned to be as I grew up in order to fit in and gain approval. The world of the masculine is spirit striving to rise ever higher. But I had discovered the wounded masculine. His use of power was subversive. I had touched also an aspect of the positive masculine. He was the hero, the adventurer. With his courage I could face more of my demons. But his spirit had been doused as a child and he had grown within my shadow, leading me to have a very negative view of masculine energy. It seemed to me that the many dreams and images I had been experiencing, filled with battle scenes and wars were some aspect of my masculine energies, which lay in the shadow. They were so fierce and troubling that I would have done anything to ignore them. I judged them as evil. But they would not go away. However the power or energy of this shadow contained the genesis of the healed masculine. He would only reveal his shadow as the feminine energy could lovingly access him. I was also beginning to realise that the power of this energy, love, could accept what I saw as the most heinous of sins. I was beginning to touch and understand the truth of unconditional love; the power to look unflinchingly at what I judged as unacceptable in myself and in the world. That was my task. But, of course, my ever-present unconscious mind continued to be judge and jury.

I reflected on the legacy of my father and his ancestors in the hope of gaining more insight into the nature of the masculine. A Women's Gathering at Magdalen Farm, facilitated by Jan Angelo, took me deeper into the feminine. Our task was to honour in ceremony our Earth Walk as women. These celebrations led me to explore the messages whispered by snake. In Native American spirituality its medicine brings the power of transformation. Poisons on all levels can be transmuted through the shedding of the snake's skin; the death of the old and the rebirth of the new. After my return from the Women's Gathering, I was taken, again through my writing, to the time of my sister's death and the unearthing of long held memories of our relationship.

Willie Gordon's Line

My father lies attached to tubes and machines. A pump keeps him alive. Although it's a bleak February day thirteen years ago, I could still be sitting next to him while white walls gleam in the dusk. The light over the bed casts faint shadows. On the other side of the Intensive Care Unit, a television set flickers ghostly pictures of Challenger as it explodes in the lower reaches of space. Disaster envelopes seven human beings, including the first woman to fly in the citizen of space programme race. Her dreams perish in the sky, while mine seem to be on hold as my father hovers between life and death.

Just a few days ago I visit him. He sits in his camel dressing gown beside his bed in the grim Victorian hospital. Doubled over, gasping for breath. On his lap lies a copy of *The Daily Telegraph*, ever a bone of contention between us!

'How are you Dad?'

'Not so bad, not so good.'

I have met this blank wall before.

'What d'you think of this?' He is pointing to a story on the front page about some exploit or other of the conservative government of Mrs. Thatcher.

The following day, his heart is attacked. My mother, who is still alive at this time, says yes, and the doctors attach him to a life-support machine to tide him through.

'A good chance he'll survive to live a fairly normal life,' the doctors say.

He is seventy-nine. I come after work to sit with him in the Intensive Care Unit.

'Hello Dad. How are you?'

There's no response.

'I've been chairing a promotion board today. I don't think you'd have approved of some of the female candidates. They were wearing trousers.'

No response. No squeeze of his hand in mine. I sit in silence. No, that's not right. Machines pump, bleep, squeak, ceaselessly. This might be another spaceship. A doctor arrives. He looks at all the charts, reads the dials and gauges. These reveal what he needs to know. Finally, he looks at the patient.

'How is he doing today, doctor?'

'Well, he's holding his own. We're going to try and wake him up tomorrow. To see if he can breathe on his own.'

The next day Dad opens his eyes. They scream silently. *He can't see. Where are his glasses?* He doesn't know us. He struggles to breathe. He can't. The doctors send him back to sleep.

He's moved to another hospital, another intensive care unit. And more days pass as he lies steeped in unconsciousness.

I realise I know so little about my father. He rarely talks about himself or the family he's come from. I take up his father's tattered scrapbook bequeathed to me by Dad's brother, Roy. It holds press cuttings announcing births, deaths, marriages of family and friends as well as details of significant events and poems. I've had it for a while and never looked at it.

Born 24th June 1906, elder son of Katie and David Robert (known as D.R.) a poem, published in the local Welsh newspaper just after his birth, extols the virtues of newly arrived Willie Gordon. Named William after his grandfather, as was the custom. I don't know where Gordon, the name he has always been known by, and the second name of his eldest grandson, Rich, comes from. It seems to have been a break with tradition. A photo as a baby shows round face, hair just the faintest sheen on his head, eyes light-coloured. They were blue-grey. He's propped against some cushions.

A postcard, sent in 1908, shows the two-year old sitting on the back of an upright chair, dressed in pale pleated skirt topped by knitted jumper. On his feet sturdy, dark lace up boots. He looks seriously into the camera from under the brim of a black hat. On the back D. R. writes, "Mrs Jones and her son are in the pink, especially the latter". My father once wore a skirt as a toddler. How distant was his childhood to him? It certainly is to me.

A year later, he wears a dark sailor suit, sporting the blonde locks his mother could not bear to have cut off. She keeps one curl in a locket in her handbag until the day she dies. He speaks only Welsh until it is time to go to school. Then it's banned from the house. English only is spoken for he has to be ready to understand in the new place of learning. He never speaks the language of his forefathers again.

Standard one, Cefn Coed School, age seven, he stands, un-smiling, arms tightly folded and wearing another sailor suit. It jolts my memory. I remember him saying, that when he was young he longed to join the Navy. At age sixteen he tried but he was colour blind. There is to be no adventure for him on the high seas. A dream, born young, is dashed.

At eight a very serious boy, mouth turned down at the corners, chin lifted high as though looking down on the world.

At nine, curls are shorn, and spectacles rest on his nose. How long has he been shortsighted? Sailor suits have disappeared. Here he is with his brother and grandmother. I have never heard him speak of her, though she doesn't die until he is eleven.

In 1920, at the age of fourteen, he sits with his family in a single-decker, open-top bus in Bournemouth. Fourteen years on, he returns with my mother for their honeymoon. Fifty years later, she is to find the hotel bill for their stay lodged in his desk drawer. She's surprised. Ah, I sense a hidden streak of sentimentality my father has rarely shown.

Football is the passion of the boy and man. Here he is, goalkeeper of Merthyr Town football team. Whenever he watches a football match on T.V., his feet go through the moves on the pitch of the carpet beneath them.

I don't have any memory of my father's presence until I am about nine or ten years. Before that time I can't hear his voice or smell him or see him. I can't remember what it feels like to be held in his arms. My reason tells me he must have been there. But for me he is absent. When do I remember him?

I'm in the first form at Grammar School tangling with Geometry. He can't help, except he finds someone who can. I decide I don't want to be like my mother and I don't want a life like hers. My father becomes my hero. I will have a life like his. His way will lead me out of the darkness of the womb-like home. But there's a price I pay. I remember I am about fourteen. We're about to move to a new house. I don't want to leave this home, the only one I've ever known. But I tell nobody; and they don't ask my opinion. I'm sent to cut the grass in the garden. I storm up and down, pushing the mower, harbouring my murderous thoughts, *This will be the last time I mow this lawn. Next time someone else will do it. This is where I've lived all my life. I don't want to go. I'll be leaving everything behind. I don't want someone else living here.* Tears roll down my face and I start to sob.

My father coming home from work asks, 'What's wrong with you?'

'I don't want to leave my home.'

'Don't be silly.' His voice is mocking. Part of me remembers him as a kind man. But this other part remembers his cutting sarcasm at the hint of any feelings. *I am afraid of this in him. I've hidden from it for a very long time.*

But still he's my hero. He was the father who, when I was crawling around the floor as a baby, threw himself on top of me as bombs fell, shattering the windows of our house. I know so little about him though. Baptised a Methodist to follow in his ancestors' footsteps. When he marries my mother, a Roman Catholic, it's a mixed marriage. This sounds strange now, as though they had different coloured skins. Married in a Catholic Church, I don't know whether he ever enters the Church again, except for weddings and funerals. He doesn't come with us to Mass on Sundays, though he always drives us there and collects us one hour later. Could a church to which he doesn't belong have any validity for me the child? All I know is that I couldn't wait to detach myself from it. As part of the marriage deal he agrees to us children being brought up as Catholics. He resists the nuns who demand we go to the schools of the faith. But instead we have to go to Saturday catechism classes, as well as Sunday School. This feels like betrayal. Does he have any beliefs about God? It seems he doesn't. Has he lost or not found the faith of his forebears?

Wesleyan Methodism is handed down through the ages. It's all here in the scrapbook. D.R., my grandfather, joins the Band of Hope at age thirteen, forswearing intoxicating drink. When I'm little, I think D.R. a posh way of saying 'Dear'. I sit on Grandpa's lap feeling the rumble of his voice when he reads my favourite stories. Even when I can read, I pretend I can't just to sit close to him. The "Loving Word" pasted in his scrapbook exhorts "Speak gently to the young, for they will have enough to bear." He holds nearly all the offices a layman can in the world of Methodism. He doesn't seek high places though. He's a collector of taxes whom the public regard as a most understanding and helpful friend. His is the first death I'm aware of. I'm thirteen. I visit him. He's returned from hospital after a heart attack. The bed's been brought downstairs and he lies on his side. He's asleep. I'm so disappointed. He won't know I've been here. He dies a few days later. Nobody tells me he might. I don't go to the funeral. I'm not even asked. As I remember this, I know it is my mother's way. Children have to be sheltered from pain, suffering and death. They are what I would like to shelter from.

William Jones, D. R.'s father, and my great-grandfather, comes from the wilds of rural Cardiganshire. In his twenties he moves to Merthyr with his wife, Anne, and becomes a pillar of Shiloh chapel. He is Choirmaster there for twenty years and the first layman to be elected to the Wesleyan Conference. He fathers thirteen children but only nine survive into adulthood. Tattered burial certificates show Elizabeth, six months; Margaret Emily, six months; Caroline Letitia, three months; Hugh William, four years; Clara, fifteen years. Where does his sadness go? In 1895, William, aged fifty, and Anne leave for Newry in Ireland. Harried out of the chapel by the extreme temperance society because he's the manager of a wine and spirits store. Is his heart broken? His father, my great-great-grandfather, Thomas is first a hatter, then a commercial traveller in tea, becomes a grocer and finally, when the post comes to Taliesin, his home village, the postmaster. In his teens he converts from Calvinism to Wesleyanism because 'Christ died for everybody, not just the chosen.' His father disowns him. Thomas the Post is a pillar of the community. His delivery round each day is very slow. He stops at the bridge over the river, outside various houses, in front of the chapel, to say his prayers. Everyone in trouble turns to him. The godless and the naughty children fear him. He preaches, raising hopes to the highest pinnacles of glory where angels sit at the right hand of God in the hereafter. Then shatters their dreams with pictures of hell, its fires burning sulphur. His wife Sarah is a zealot. What a heady mix. But is their faith born of love or fear?

Does my father know all this? Does he learn it at his father's knee? If he does, he remains silent on the matter for me. But I sense this strand of Methodism arriving in me to mix with the

Roman Catholicism of my mother's family. I have been instilled with the beliefs of a masculine-dominated Christianity from which the spirit of the feminine has been exiled. Not even the religious fervour of my father's great-grandparents is apparent in my father. But I wonder. All his life I recall he suffers with migraine. What lies buried I wonder.

I will never know for he dies in the intensive care unit taking his secrets with him. I will have to find my own way through the yoke of my raped spirituality.

Red Moon

Sixteen women prepare for their first-ever Red Moon Gathering. It's the month of June. I'm organising my ceremonial outfits just as the other participants are. I imagine a spectator watching and wondering what is happening. We besiege Charity Shops and scour rails for dresses, skirts, blouses, trousers, whilst chanting, *Red Moon, Red Moon. Oh Yes, Red Moon. Thank you.* The volunteer workers don't know what the Red Moon is, but they see its power reflected in our dedicated seekers' thanks for the addition of any small item to our collections. Dress, craft, fabric, and crystal shops are not exempt from attention. Lengths of material, feathers, ribbons, beads, rattles, gems, jewellery, scarves disappear from shelves as fast as they can be re-stocked. Nobody watching knows when or where we Red Moon Women will descend. Our successful searches aren't limited to the colour red. Yellow, white and black are just as significant in our findings. Jan Angelo, the facilitator of the Gathering, has asked us to bring four outfits in each of these colours. Encouraged by our enthusiasm and dedication, one shop assistant sees that some of us are extremely reluctant when it comes to certain colours, particularly yellow. Most of us claim it doesn't suit us. She tells us it's last year's black. That often does the trick.

The Clan Mother for the month of June is "Storyteller". Illusions can be untangled when we place ourselves in our hearts. We sixteen women are assembled at Magdalen Farm on the first evening. In the company of the other women in the circle, my imagination takes me to the cave of the lower belly. My task is to cleanse it. Pale light throws faint shadows on part scrubbed walls as I enter. My eyes roam around accustoming themselves to the dimness. Thick brown and green moss streaks across alcoves and water streams in rivulets across the cobbled floor. At the centre of the cavern a small fire smoulders, its smoke curling up and around into secret niches. I clean out the hearth, raking grey and silver ashes to one side and fan gently red embers. Flames lick and spurt from the shadows to illuminate gleaming black jet encrusted in the sides of this chamber deep underground. I smooth its outer skin, a coat of snakeskin; against its side, winged arms layered with white feathers. A golden crown glints through its red hair. I contemplate the gift I bring to the gathering. It is freedom. With my fellow celebrants I sing to the four directions.

The scene is set for us to sit in circle over the next few days in each of the four directions. In the East, the incoming spirit of fire enters life. Here lives the Goddess in me, the Visionary, the Seer who ushers into this world the divine spark birthing all my impressions, feelings, sensations, dreams whether I notice them or not. My robe is golden yellow and I celebrate her arrival on my earth walk. Nine times I circle the altar in carefree dance, chanting silently my intention to free my spirit and to help all women to do the same. I come to rest in my place, full of joyful anticipation. The internal voice unearths its clamour.

What you've done is not good enough. You were having such a good time, you forgot your intention. You don't deserve to get anywhere.

I halt the voice and wait. Another slinks into view.

It's not possible to do or get what I want. It's not possible to find the passion of the East.

The fiery image subsides and smoulders. My shoulders sag in despair.

I am the Woman Child of the South wearing a red sari. The altar holds photographs of each woman present, of her as a child. In mine, I sit with my sister, Sue. The spirit children are invited into our circle and they file in to dance before the altar or to rest or play. I sense that neither my sister's nor mine will enter to sit with me. Perhaps they hover at the gateway. There is space for them but they cannot take their places. There are so many children here but not mine, it seems.

In black, I journey to celebrate the Dreaming Woman of the West. Here I call upon the spirit of Pele, the Goddess of the greatest volcano on the Island of Hawaii. In her physical body she erupts molten lava from the centre of her earthen body. From her emotional world she spews material from the shadow into the light. Her energy is fire; she resents control or domination. She must speak her truth no matter what reaction it gives rise to. In my imagination, her energy travels through my body as a snake, stealing from the cave of the lower belly along my spine, threading through vertebrae until she emerges through my throat to rest on my left cheek. I sense she whispers messages, trickling across my skin. I will have to wait to understand them.

In the North, the place of the grandmothers, in my white outfit, I celebrate the place of wisdom. Across the circle facing me, I sense that the wisdom of this direction can show me yet more about the woman child who faces me in the South. The Guardian of Medicine Stories has much to show me; of how I can listen again to the child, without judgement and unhelpful advice for she has yet more secrets to impart. Until she does, I sense that the battle to reveal my spirit in all that I do will continue. But this Clan Mother can push me beyond my stubbornness.

Dreaming Woman's Gift

One by one, crisply yellowed leaves slide from the Magnolia tree in my garden, rustling to a soft landing on the earth below. Warm autumn day is turning into raw evening as dusk speeds in. I've been writing about my sister, Sue again, pondering over just what it is I want to say. *Will spring ever come again? Surely the newly bared branches are sprouting buds before their time. Is it too soon for them to survive winter's frosts and snows? No. Their coats of velvet fur, tightly wrapped, will cloak them until spring comes.* As I wait with these idle thoughts, Jupiter appears in the sky and the beginning of an ancient sadness germinates in my body.

I trace it through the passages of memory to an autumn day nineteen years ago and I go into my study to write.

We're watching our aunts bury bulbs of scarlet tulip and golden daffodil in the border on the other side of the window. My sister will not see their flowering in the spring. The cancer grows relentlessly. It has her in its grip. She is fading slowly but surely. There are not many weeks left for her here. We do not speak of her death, but we know it. I still can't find a place in me in which to accommodate it. I am without a map to navigate my way through these waters. She is too. She is one month short of forty-one years.

The sadness of that moment rises up within me now, as I write, just as a spring rises in the heart of a mountain to stream into a river, into an ocean. My tears flow. What if Sue was here now? I can't bear to think how it would be. Would we be standing in the garden laughing, talking? What about? My imagination won't swing into action. In all my grieving these are the things I've never asked myself, so I've never heard any answers. I think of what it would be for her sons, husband, mother, father. I don't know how to think about it because if my sister were still here I would not be the person I am now. And I can't bear to think of that because I would have missed so much of the self I've come to know since she died. But I can't stop myself crying. This morning I open the front door on my way to work and, for just one second, a wild desperation fills my body until it shakes itself through disjointed limbs into feelings, thoughts. There is nowhere I can go where

I am in my life; inside is no safer than outside. This is the day my sister died nineteen years ago. The disconnection of unknowing passes. How strange that I am more comfortable with knowing for a moment that I feel I am leaving my life, than with not knowing. There is more to remember of that time when my life changed forever. To hear, what I dared not hear then. I continue to write.

'Sue might have cancer. Again.'

I'm standing in the hall of my mother's house, hairbrush in my hand, as she tells me the news. The silent cells banished by the surgeon's knife two years earlier may have continued their stealthy invasion. This knowledge cleaves through my body. A door is pushed ajar, but I cannot enter. It must not stay open. Unaware of any thought screaming 'close it', I hurl it shut. Now other memories filter in. Sue, pale and pinched of face, folded inside herself, sits on a deckchair in the middle of the sitting room of this house I've just bought. Cold rises from a new concrete floor, bare of rugs or carpet. A working party paints, papers and hammers. She wants to be in the middle of the activity, but cannot be part of it. It's lunchtime. I give her a bowl of soup, a sandwich. She hardly touches them. She is to go into hospital for tests tomorrow. We speak words I don't remember, and I hold her hand.

The next day I loiter in a hospital corridor watching, through a window, wild clouds pushing on to the east. Smells of sickly polish, sharp disinfectant and bodily wastes and decay fill the trapped air. Outside the sun is shining. Inside, I inhabit a greyly dense world. I turn as the ward sister calls me to come. The doctor has left the bedside. Sue sits on the high hospital bed, tears coursing down her face. I sit next to her and hold her hands. The news is not good.

'I do have cancer of the liver. Need to have chemotherapy. Thirty per cent chance of a remission.'

For how long I wonder

'How will Mike cope? What about the children?'

I cry with her.

'I'm going to fight this.'

'I'm with you.' What that means I don't know. But I will be. Can I cry and be strong? I've never been in a place like this. How can we be here where death lurks? There's been no rehearsal for this foreign place. For the moment tears are spent.

'Do you know what I want?'

'What? Tell me! What ever it is, I'll get it.'

'Beetroot and potato sandwiches. I'm starving.'

We laugh at the remembered food of childhood. Thoughts of death can be defeated with food…. for the present.

As I sit here remembering and writing, an old chest floats down to rest at my feet. Its wood is mahogany; brass hinges and lock are rusted and stiff. Keen-eyed Hawk circles above, watching, waiting as I decide which memories I will unship from this wooden cavern. His piercing cry tells me that what I take out cannot be returned and what I put in, cannot be retrieved. I must be willing to face what I have judged. I lift the lid. Lying across the top is a photograph album, faded and worn. Its corners crumble as I open the blue cover...

And here we are Sue, sitting together for a long series of miniature photos. In each, we pose differently, at least I do. Smiling, laughing, pulling faces, interested, bored. You look composed. You're about four, me two. We're wearing the dresses Mum smocked through the long nights of the war. Mine has red thread, yours blue. You are a white-haired angel, not a strand out of place. Serenely, you gaze ahead holding me with both arms as though it is the only way I can be kept in my place. Maybe I haven't learned to be quiet and still.

Here we are; my first term in primary school. I'm four and you're six. Your hair, grown darker, is plaited and wrapped around your head. My mouth is shut tightly. I've been missing my two front teeth ever since I slipped and knocked them out on the front door step more than a year ago. 'Too much excitement before a dancing display,' Mum said. Remember those days when, in between chanting the times table, we are trailed around the teachers for them to admire Mum's needlework? They say to you, 'How pretty you are.' They don't say it about me, so I know I'm not. But I learn it's important to be pretty. That's how you get noticed. I don't know what makes you it and me not. Whatever it is, I long for it. The most I remember is Dad once saying about me, 'She's not a bad looking kid – when she smiles.' I try it for a while but it doesn't match the inside.

Here we are on the beach at Broadhaven in West Wales, on holiday. Sitting inside the walls of the sandcastle we've built, waiting for the sea to come in and wash our handiwork away. I don't remember this time. 'You played together when you were small,' Mum said. 'No arguing, no fighting. You were very good.' It's lost in the mists of time. We were not allowed to argue or fight, I'm sure. It doesn't sound natural somehow. I wonder what you remember?

You're behind the camera for this one. I'm nine, wearing a red and white check dress. We're just back from holiday in Cornwall, browned by endless days of hot sunshine. This is the year you disappear from me. We build no sandcastles on the beach nor play rounders or cricket. Your head is buried in a book from one day's end to the other. I am desolate. I don't know what's happened. You don't respond to any of my pleas to hold back the tide behind walls of sand. You go from me. Are we ever such companions again? What have I done wrong?

Here you are, the Queen of the fete in our home village. Chosen from how many young girls, I don't know. Attendants surround you, though I'm not one of them. I can't compete. Saturday night dances. How I envy you, men flocking to you drawn by I don't know what while I'm the traditional wallflower. You tell me it's my fault for looking so stuck up. Fear and shame are the feelings inside me. Jealousy of you streaks through me now, surprising me with its strength and depth. It separates me from you. Are you jealous of me? If you are, will that make me feel better? No wonder I can't make a place inside me for your death. Part of me has to die now. The guilt of the crippled "Claudia" for harbouring such thoughts must die.

You don't know why you had to die. I don't know either. I've always thought it should have been me. But it was you who was chosen and not me. That is how it is. This is the Great Mystery. No scientist can explain it no matter how he might try. So I say I thank God for your life and for your dying otherwise I would have remained ignorant and unknown to myself.

For now I can tell no more of this story. It's too painful and I'm not ready to go wherever I have to.

Chapter Ten

Remember Me

Chapter Ten

Remember Me

In the seven years since I had attended the healing and the chakra workshops I had continued to retrieve much of my inner life, which I had put away as a child. But Earthworm, who I had come so near to rejecting, had helped me to bring to the surface the feelings of envy and jealousy, which I had labelled as some of the most unacceptable feelings. I didn't realise that they are part of what it is to be a human being; that they can, and often are, part of the lot of siblings. But they had stood in the way of my truly grieving for the loss of my sister. They were not to be given up easily for, as with all the feelings carried from childhood, they had formed a firm basis for the way I viewed life and how I related to it. I was being invited to dive deeper into the mysteries of the soul.

Over the coming months, the still to be revealed messages continued to stop me in my tracks. The writer called it her block. So did the singer. Both became activities I found it increasingly difficult to engage with. But both had to be my way through days of depression and out into the world. At a local arts centre a friend, with whom I had been working on my writing, invited me to read some of my writing and follow it with an improvised song to raga Bhairavi. A few months later I embarked on learning more about the techniques of singing raga. This is a skill, which Indian classical singers spend years and years learning and mastering. Each raga has its own flavour created by the specific notes it contains. Although the ongoing Voice and Movement Course had introduced us to the basic elements of the form and techniques, some of our group began to come together to learn more of the intricacies of singing raga. And this is when Gilles Petit introduced us to the raga known as Gunakali.

Not long before the moon's eclipse of the sun in the UK, I attended a retreat, led by Jack Angelo, at which we explored more of the nature of the partnership between the masculine and the feminine. At another Red Moon Gathering of Women, we celebrated the spiritual power of women. Although I didn't understand it at the time, my search for and discovery of the feminine was revealing not only the wounded masculine but also that my feminine had exiled my lost hero. He must be brought out of exile and this meant answering the call for more travel adventure. I took myself off to Africa again, walking in Swaziland, an independent kingdom within the boundaries of South Africa, and then over the border into Mpumalanga, the most northeasterly province of South Africa.

Waxing and Waning

Week after week, a race of demons locks my limbs with iron bars so that muscles wither and wane. I stretch my arms to touch thoughts, to hold them in my hands, but they spin out of control, evading capture. Their threads draw me down into the room of the traitorous womb lying in the shadow of the eternal hangman. Blood that was red turns into rivers of brown sediment. All that has been denied by the executioner spews forth. Raging in my body, spinning, chasing, charging; cursing through the entrails of my stomach bringing with her the bile of centuries through choked channels on the weight-less power of my breath. Without knowing her, this vengeful hag exists across bare mountains through icy streams. Now I must recall her. But this body she inhabits is too fragile to contain her within its skin of stretched silk. My body is not safe to live in.

♫

I've read Waxing and Waning. Now comes the really challenging bit for me. I'm going to improvise to raga Bhairavi. The notes are 'Sa', '<u>Re</u>', '<u>Ga</u>', 'Ma', 'Pa', '<u>Da</u>', '<u>Ni</u>', 'Sa'. Underlining of the notes means that they are flattened.

I wait for the audience to settle. I'm sitting cross-legged on a small stage my harmonium propped on the floor and one knee. At a short rehearsal before the performance begins, the organisers agree with me that I do not need the microphone. Thank goodness. I know my voice will reach easily all corners of the room. My task is to keep it in tune. I look out across the darkened room and over the heads of the seated audience. I can see two men standing at the back of the room leaning against the bar. They are chatting. My stomach turns over. *This is going to be awful. Is this what nightclub performers feel like? Well I won't look at them, but I'll sing to them.* I squeeze the harmonium, which sets the drone playing my 'Sa'. I settle my voice into it. And then introduce each note joining it with its predecessors before moving on. Gradually, the men at the back of the room disappear from my attention. And I relax into the notes. And without my noticing, I am singing but it is as though my voice is no longer mine. It flows from somewhere other than me. I am no longer thinking which note shall I reach next. And everyone in the room no longer exists until the voice ceases. One man tells me that he could have listened forever.

Who sings?

Consolation

All Wild Child Woman asks are you there Ma?
No reply.

Now Ma is the mother full of colour both lighter and darker
of mating creating birthing and dying.
Meandering and mewling All Wild Child Woman
misses the Ma.

She howls and she moans for she's full of the woe
of no Ma for now.

The notes of raga Gunakali are 'Sa', '<u>Re</u>' , 'Ma', 'Pa', '<u>Da</u>', 'Sa'. There is no Ga or Ni. This collection of notes and their relationship to each other is what distinguishes Gunakali from any other raga. Traditionally it's sung at daybreak.

Gunakali, the colours of the great Hindu Goddess of the many hands. Dishevelled Kali, holding aloft her club to slash away the useless, the old, the dead; her staff to dispel the fear of these actions. In her bowl she carries her spiritual force from deep within her body to dance upon the corpse of her husband; moving her energy to bring him to life. I set out to create my feeling shape of her raga from the within of my body.

I light the sound with my 'Sa', touching, honing until it swims through corpuscles reddening rich.

I slide the air on muscles down through the throat to graze '<u>Da</u>'. I give it no name and return as the blunt side of a knife slides gently stretching skin across flesh to the 'Sa' of no name.

I skim back to '<u>Da</u>' naming it before I arrive at its door. I open it wider tasting for ripeness of the autumn blackberry and then return once more to settle in my expansive 'Sa'.

From here my voice slides down to fill the cells through '<u>Da</u>' unnamed to 'Pa'. I pour my sound deep into earth and name it. I glide through '<u>Da</u>' coiling through 'Sa' to taste the dull orange flesh of '<u>Re</u>' unnamed and slide back to 'Sa'.

Then the same again but naming the '<u>Re</u>'. Now from '<u>Da</u>' to '<u>Re</u>' and on to a hint of 'Ma'. But her colour and flavour evade my capture.

The tears from within the feeling body wait no longer. This raga offers the consolation of the life of the Great Mother. Her arms could hold me as no earthly arms can. And so I explore, hesitatingly, the colours of Kali. But her sound will not enfold me. Why this is so, is not for me to know at this moment but to experience in the feeling of my body. The yearning and longing for a home I cannot remember. For now, it is enough to know of this possibility.

Sun and Moon

Twisted twigs of blackened bark
stand stark in dawns bloody reds.
Mighty pygmies lost in mire
make wounds to silence hearts.

There they are. Two bodies hanging in the heavens separated not by time but by space. Until they must meet. The opalescent pearl gown in which she sails through some of my days is fuzzy, insubstantial, just hinting at the subtle splendour of her night array. Only then is her light visible as it shines white in the dark hours making seen what is invisible. He, in his peacock gold, strides through my blue days, illuminating with the myriad colours of the rainbow. Neither is meant to meet until the heavens right themselves and she sails across his face to mask his gleam, paling it with the torments of night. Why she has come to eclipse him now, the scientist can explain. But he knows not that the time signals a meeting such as is rarely known on this earth in these days. It trumpets loud the call for the sharing of a power that the elders speak of but which we, their descendants, ignore. In her left hand, she carries her bowl containing all that speaks of her life past, present and future here on earth. In that grail lies all that is needed to guide his actions away from violence, fear, hatred. This is the chalice, which says yes to self, but not in a selfish way. He approaches with his sword held in his right hand ready to deter, to say 'no' to all that will come from another to strike her down. He is the gatekeeper through which all that would violate her must be turned back and through which he must usher her deepest secrets and wishes into this world. In partnership they dance their spiral, twisting, turning a romance of skeins that speaks of the power of love rather than the love of power. Mark them; note them; for together they can be denied no longer.

Stake your life on them.

I journey to visit my wounded Moon and Sun. They must be disinterred. She dances, whirling wildly. Her drum beats out the rhythm of her heart's flame seeking a way into the arena of the sunlit world. The gates are closed. He is the one to open them. She cannot do it without him. In her dress of greens and blues, hair flying in the zephyr breezes, she beckons me nearer. 'Let me out,' she laments; the madness of grief clogs up her gyrating body.

But where is he?

Into parched labyrinth I follow a trail traced through the sands of timeless desert. My footfalls echo ahead, beneath, above and behind. The dry dust of days, months, years, centuries hangs captured in windless passageways. Webs of spider hang from ribs of dulled wood. Here, there is no golden laughter, no song. No whispers stir air. At the heart of these secret vaults, I arrive at a marble tomb raised above the ground. Upon it, a warrior lies motionless. His body, unmarked by visible wounds, cannot be roused. His mummified mouth shields his muteness.

'How much longer will you languish here? Can you not raise yourself?' My cries echo through canals of deaf years.

A tear trickles across his pallid cheek. 'I am laid low by the narrow vision of old.'

Could he be my hero?

Return of the Red Moon

We are "Women in Search of the Sacred", ready to celebrate the spiritual power of women. There's something different here. We are speaking of spirit. Is this something different from soul? Maybe I am going to find out, for the questions for this second Red Moon Gathering are moving into yet more aspects of feminine power. Who am I? There's that question again. How am I connected to all things in the universe? And this year, the time of the total eclipse, when the moon will come to sit in the lap of the sun, is approaching. It signifies the time for the feminine to share power with the masculine; to acknowledge Mary Magdalen as the Bride of Christ, the un-crowned Queen of the Heavens and the marriage of heaven and earth, of body with spirit.

In ceremony, dressed in the greening of the Earth Mother, I enter the fifth direction on the Wheel of Life, the Below. The place of the lower three chakras, the base, sacral and solar plexus. It's time for more healing. Deer enters my meadow bringing her medicine of tender compassion. Oh, I need to look at the way I treat myself. 'How are you tough on yourself?' she asks, as she lifts her head to gaze at me.

Feathered Dog flies through my vision. 'Have you respect for, trust in and intimacy with yourself?' I know I have not, still. And so I cannot have them in my relationships with others.

Eel swims through the waters of my body with its electric medicine. 'Remember, through the pain lies the love which is all encompassing, doesn't judge and can make things right without waiting.' Will I ever cease to find fault with myself?

Now I hold the Mother's stone in my left hand and hear what she has to tell me. Tested in the fires of living I am battle scarred. Fissures criss-cross my face and holes mark my surface sprinkled with embedded crystals gleaming in the sun. Buried in my body, yet more crystals. Has there ever been a time when I haven't felt unblemished, unscarred by wounds unhealed? Wailing and groaning and screaming pour forth from the bowels of my earth. And with one change of thought and one re-vision I sing of the beauty captured through and around my crevices.

That night, I dream.

I am crawling through a maze of bodies slumped across a battlefield. Soldiers all. I am the only one alive. Crazy metal lightning blazes across night. It lights up a pearly banner hung in the sky with one word in black emblazoned upon it. Magic. Below, circus performers with painted and lipsticked faces, tumble through the midst of lion and elephant. Caught in a brilliant spotlight, a girl in white tutu spins and twirls atop the bare back of a cantering palomino.

The following morning, I fly to the Blue Above, the sixth direction on the Wheel of Life, the home of the sky nation, the throat, brow and crown chakras. Through waters turned purple by her ink, Octopus' eight arms envelope me in the healing powers of love, reminding me to give thanks for every healing step I take. Otter plays in the waters with innocence and delight and in the sky, Hummingbird flits from bloom to bloom tasting the joy of nectar in all human experience. Spider Woman crawls through my hair and enters my body weaving her hinged legs through it, just as at the dawn of life she spins her silver threads from her own dreaming. Her strands weave my creation through me. Her web travels through the somnolent air and I see it join me, in turn, to all the women lying in this circle and to the skeins of prayer ties, which join us to our altar offerings. Later, we paint a spider's web on each of our faces and circle our dance of creation around the burning fire beneath the stars.

♫

On Sunday, I sit in the Within Place, where the heart lies at the centre of the Wheel of Life, balancing all that is below with all that is above. This is the place of faith in the Great Mystery of life. Faith. The word reminds me that if there is a word then its state must exist. It must be possible to know it in myself. Tears damned by a thought of no faith break loose to wash away yet more rubble from the interior. I might now be able to find the tracks left by the walking sticks across the trails I follow in my dreams. Thunderbird approaches with the clapping rolls of thunder to show how my heart has chilled. And now I reach beyond that memory, wondering when the leaves will change and when SHE, the divine feminine presence of Kabbalah, will return. The Shekinah who lives clothed in the black of lamentations for her son child. Her light has been dimmed for thousands of years as she mourns his absence.

Land of Rising Sun

9 a.m. Johannesburg airport. I was last here thirty-three years ago, waiting for a connecting flight, just as I am now. Then I spent most of my time working out which was the correct toilet to use. Only one, of the six, was legal for a white woman. The building I remember then was grey, utilitarian and joyless. Today it's bustling and filled with sunshine. Thirty-three years ago, I travelled with my eldest sister, Annie, who was living here for a short time, from one end of the country to the other in her elderly Ford Prefect car.

'What do you think of our country?' her white South African friends would ask me.

'The country is very beautiful. But none of you are free.'

'But we are. We can go where we wish, meet who we wish, do as we wish.'

'No you can't. You can't marry a black person. They can't live where they choose. How can you endure all this comfort while they live in poverty — and make life luxurious for you?'

'But you don't understand.' And so the long litany, justifying their way of life would begin.

Now I catch my connecting flight to Manzini in Swaziland, where I meet up with the fifteen other people whom I hike with in some of the National Reserves of the country. From there we cross into South Africa for more walking and some times watching animals. As we drive to our hotel, through towns straggling along main roads, we pass dozens of funeral parlours. The death toll here from AIDS, as in Swaziland, continues to grow.

Eye to eye with mighty buffalo. She rests on her haunches. I hear her pant and snort. My breath comes in short spurts. She is resting, maybe waiting. With head down she could charge at any moment, enraged by these interlopers. We've been walking for over an hour in this cool part of the morning.

Camouflaged by tall sprouting umbrella thorns, three giraffe watch us set off in the wake of two guides. We are looking for signs of a rhinoceros and her baby seen nearby yesterday. We trek through folded thickets, crouched low until a narrow dirt trail opens before us. The way is littered with the fresh aroma of buffalo droppings. We string out, bush rising thick around and above. Through bare branches I see one massive black beast. She lies about a hundred metres from me. Crouching close to the ground our group blocks the way of the herd to fresh pasture and water. They are waiting to cross this narrow track on which I kneel. Blue Buffalo Woman, the name given to me three years earlier at a Sweat Lodge, swims across my vision. Her blueness then is of the hazy distance suggesting I need to draw her gifts nearer to me. Her medicine is prayer and praise for all that has been received. She teaches that when gratitude is expressed to every living part of creation, abundance becomes available. Here, today, I am face-to-face with the live creature. I bow my head to her and give thanks for all her gifts. It's time to leave, to allow the herd to move on its way. We turn and head into even deeper bush to meet with the rhinoceros and her infant.

This is Mpumalanga, the Land of the Rising Sun. It lies in the north- east of South Africa. On its low veld, forty thousand years ago, the stone age San people roam. In trance, dance and song they celebrate their connection with the spirit world, through nature. This is their home long before the black tribes of North Africa push south and drive them into the Kalahari Desert. To the west, the land rises to form the lip of an Escarpment in the Drakensburg Mountains. It is here where the low veld meets the high veld that I return to the ravine and descend to its base. To reach it, I cross the Treur River where in 1844 Voortrekker men leave their women and children and set out to find a way to the coast in the East. A month later the women, thinking them dead, leave in sorrow after naming the river. Three days later the men return to find their families camping, this time, by a river they name Blyde. Where these two rivers the Sorrow and the Happiness meet, I look down into cauldrons of rock carved by tempestuous waters over millions of years.

From here we enter the beginnings of a canyon gouged from the earth's crust by the humble Blyde. My boots scrape through crumbling earth the colour of rusty nails. Underneath, lies smooth, glistening, rose pink clay. Down a track, roughly hewn by the footsteps of beast and then man, I push through the thick foliage of heavily laden trees. In cliffs high above, monkeys swing with vigour between overhanging branches. The path twists and turns on itself. My legs stretch down to reach a foothold on embedded rocks washed smooth. To my left, the ground falls away in steep slopes of loose-lying scree bedding precarious thorn bushes. It is here that one of our group looses her footing and slips from the path. Her fall is broken, several feet down the slope, by a handy thorn bush. One strong-armed male manages to hoist her back to safety. She only has a few scratches but is shaken.

'That could have been me,' I tell her. 'I'm much too busy looking at the scenery to watch my footing.'

To the right, through nestling bushes, a wall of golden rocks assembled through the ages to resemble the mighty pipes of an organ, rises to tower overhead. From shade to light and light to shade, the craggy route winds down for hours of footsteps to a disused powerhouse. Once the driving source of water needed for nearby gold mines, now closed. Standing nearby is the shuttered homestead of the onetime resident engineer and his family. From here I tread gingerly down a cobbled path spiralling almost vertically into a glade where the river has come to rest for the time being. It has taken nearly four hours to reach this wooded den where cool waters bound over flat boulders.

Just eight of our party of sixteen have come this far, descending eight hundred metres into a canyon which it has taken the Blyde waters sixty million years to carve. I am hot, weary, hungry and thirsty and blessed with a fiery rash over most of my body. Yesterday I went to the local clinic. There I was called into see a doctor, who sat me down and, before asking what the matter was said,

'What do you think of this country?'

Before I could answer he said 'We're leaving in two months, for Canada.'

'Permanently?'

'Ya. Things aren't the same anymore. I have children and the schools are no longer adequate. Too many in the classes and standards have fallen. There's much crime. It's too dangerous living here.'

The litany gets longer.

'I know it's a shame. But I have to do the best for my family.' He shrugs his shoulders as though he is helpless.

After half an hour I learn that, for the first time I'm allergic to the spring pollen.

'It's the first day of spring,' the doctor announces. He gives me ointments and tablets and I leave the surgery.

Paul, the catering manager of the hotel where we are staying, drives me back. It is only a couple of miles but apparently it would not have been safe for me to walk or come on my own.

'Is life very different for you since the free elections?'

'Oh yes. Before, I wouldn't have had a chance to train in catering let alone get a job in management.'

'Have you hope for the future?'

'Oh yes. As long as my government is allowed to do what is the best for my country. Thabo Mbeki can make a good job of improving the economy.'

I ponder on these two conversations while I eat my sandwiches at the bottom of the Blyde Canyon. I remember a third comment made to me by another man a few days ago.

'If we whites wait long enough, AIDS will decimate the country. It'll return to us then. You see.'

The breeze seems chilly suddenly.

The path before me looks as though it rises almost vertically as I chew on an apple.

'How long do you think it'll take us to get back,' I ask one of my companions.

'Five, maybe six hours.'

'It's going to be hard work.'

'It's time to go. We have to get back before the Park at the top closes at 5p.m. Otherwise, we'll be spending the night in the minibus,' our leader announces.

It's 2.30 p.m. and around the last bend Henry appears. We thought he had stayed at the old homestead. He is eighty years old and walks slowly with a stick.

'Henry. We have to start back straight away,' our leader shouts.

'That's all right. You know I don't like to stop. I just keep to my steady pace.'

Escaping from the sun wherever possible, I criss-cross from light to dark stopping at self-imposed targets of shade. At the old homestead I stand under a hosepipe. It spurts cold water over heated limbs. In just about two hours I emerge from the canyon to contemplate God's Window at the edge of the world. *How come going up is so much quicker than climbing down?* I have followed the path to my hero.

We can survive and thrive.

Chapter Eleven

The Voice

Chapter Eleven

The Voice

I pondered over this journey of mine. When I looked back to my first encounter with the ravine, eight years earlier, during the healing journey through the chakra workshops, it seemed that I had been disinterring my soul's memories. It had been serving them up to me in so many ways mystical to my rational mind, that mind which likes to control through its grip on the conventions it has honed through the years. For me, to write and sing and be in this world required the food of the soul to be served without the embellishment and censorship of the rigid rules acquired in the bloom of childhood and sharpened in the crucible of non-feeling and non-remembering. The events, the thoughts, the feelings, the sensations, the pictures, the sounds, the songs, the images had to be resurrected and entered so that extinguished life could rise from the ashes. It meant letting go of what my mind thought was perfection.

I came back from Africa feeling I had reached another layer of my healed masculine. As usual, this was the signal for a deeper plunge into the feminine. Before a walking holiday in Morocco at Christmas, I spent quite a bit of my quiet time trying to sort out what I called the God Business. In the New Year I fell headlong into a discordant world of sound. This led me into exploring, over a period of months, what death meant to me. Then in the summer, I took myself off to a Healing Sounds Intensive level II with Jonathan Goldman in Colorado.

Stormy Waters

'Woman of skin, woman of bone,
nothing gets by me you I will hone.
Doors I will open, doors I will close,
forge you and fire you
until you're full grown.'

The Crone's Song

Kay Leverton

I return from Africa and re-read a card a friend sent me before I went away. It portrays Athena, the Goddess of Wisdom, from a painting by Susan Seddon Boulet. Athena is the Greek form of the older African Goddess, Neith, the inventor of weaving and so is the patroness of the arts and weaving.

According to Greek mythology, Athena was born out of the head of her father Zeus. *That's always seemed like a pretty mad idea.* But it reminds me. Athena becomes her father's daughter. She models herself on him. *This sounds familiar.* Athena's totem animals are the Owl of Wisdom, and my old friends, the Snake of Transformation and the Spider, the Weaver. I remember reading somewhere that Athena yearns to know the unrevealed spirit.

A few days later, I dream.

I am visiting a woman in hospital. I know I've visited her several times before. I sit on her bed and as I look at her, she becomes me in the bed, and then becomes herself again. She tells me that they have found out what I need to know. A baby is due to arrive from Africa.

When I wake up, I wonder if this is the birth of the un-revealed spirit – my hero of Africa?

A few days later as I lie in the bath gazing at the mottled tiles on the wall in front of me, a face appears. It is of Christ – well it's similar to the sort of western representations of his face that appear in paintings such as Leonardo da Vinci's *Last Supper*.

I get out of the bath and write in my journal to see where all this might take me? What if I think about Jesus as I think about Mary Magdalen? She is the hidden feminine. He could be the hidden masculine. I have been jettisoning, and continue to do so, the old beliefs, some of which are still lodged in me, about the feminine and what it is to be a woman. So, I need to let go of the old beliefs I have about the masculine. How I think about God is top of the list. Because God is still a HE – the result of all patriarchal religions. This idea, that a divine being is a he, and only a he, flies in the face of all the beliefs that I am coming to know about a divine feminine being. In energy terms, a divine being must be a play, a dance between mascu-line and feminine energy. The old masculine God that I have in my head is the wounded masculine. His thoughts, beliefs, ideas and acts still seem to be alive and well in me. And they do not match up with the Christ, Son of God, who is described in the Bible. So why can't I allow Christ as the healed masculine energy into my life instead of the great judgemental being called God, who seems to deny the existence of love. I feel a life-changing insight in this and am greatly comforted by it.

A few days later, I write again in my journal. I've been watching a male friend with his mother-in-law who is in an old people's home. He treats her with warmth, care and love. When I tell him that this is what I have witnessed he denies it with the comment,

'I didn't have a good relationship with my mother.'

So does this mean that he can't have a good relationship with his mother in law? Does the masculine have to deny love in order to be masculine?

Amongst all these days of reflections, I develop a sore throat and then a full-blown cold.

'Is this some kind of release?' a friend asks.

My 'yes' slips out without thinking. How am I going to do this? As usual, I'm resisting because I'm having difficulty getting my head out of the way. It doesn't have the answer.

After weeks of squirming, I write in my journal …

My words become orphaned by storms, as I hear others

pour theirs out in rivers. My flow is choked behind a dam I have built and on the other side, that flow is diverted and leaks into the bones and muscles of my body where they lie stagnant. The bones for my writing are nowhere.

Yet this very act of writing words begins to breach the dam.

As I lay down to sleep one night I "see", with a clear vision, that I have placed everything about myself and others connected with love outside of my heart lest it break from disappointment.

For days, pain gathers in the centre of my heart, but it cannot pour out of me. It is as though this pain has mostly by-passed my heart. Now it has to pass through my heart. It comes coloured with bitterness, jealousy, envy, loss, failure. But love is uncompromising. It says, see the beauty of these feelings I have labelled scabrous. Hear why they exist. What is their conversation? But my old God says, 'No. Consign these matters to the shadows. Do not acknowledge them. They are unlovely and unlovable. I have no truck with whinings and whingeings. Get on with life.' I would like to. But there is no by-pass. I have to go through. This is the way of the Goddess, the way of care, the way of love.

My shadow God shows me guilt for having these feelings. I am stoppered up. Better not write about them. Better not sing lest they leak out. Others will read them in your words, hear them in your voice just as you read and hear them in theirs.

Despicable rage. Put it away. But it's my spirit.

My book will not be written.

It will.

I write another section.

Censor that.

No I won't.

Yes I will.

I write another section.

No.

Yes.

I'll rub your nose in it.

♫

I take myself off to wander by the river. It is full. The rains of the past few days have swollen its grey mass. It swirls, murky alongside me, travelling fast to the sea just a mile or so ahead of me.

I take myself to the sea. A gale blows as I set off to walk along the coast and the rain thrusts itself into my face. I am soaked. I return to the dry of my car and sit watching the sodden sheep, head to tail behind the wall, waiting the storm out, just as I have to.

What a relief: it's Christmas and time to go away.

Furnace of Sound

'Stylo, bonbons? Stylo, bonbons?'

We're a group of twenty trudging up a stony track into the village of Tizgui, in the foothills of the Atlas Mountains in Morocco. Children tumble down narrow rocky paths to join us. Hopping and running alongside, they chant this mantra; we hear it whenever we reach a Berber village.

'You mustn't give them any pens or sweets. It leads to bullying.' Our Berber leader is very firm on this subject.

Three bold young girls skip in step with me as I shrug my shoulders, 'Pas de stylos, pas de bonbons. Ca va?'

They continue to chant, giggling and pointing at my dangling earrings. They would like them. No more than eight or nine years old, faces smeared with mud, they wear, with unexpected elegance, a varied collation of clothes. Cotton dresses of ochre, emerald and crimson swirl over electric pink and orange leggings. Elegantly wound, fringed scarves adorn their heads and trail over their shoulders. Any model would be envious of them. Their mothers stand smiling, nodding in response to our greetings. A group of women emerge onto the track ahead of us. Strapped to their backs are piles of branches and kindling they have carried from the woods way down the hillside. Up front, Peter, one of our group, is entertaining a gathering of young boys with his version of an energetic high-jumping Russian dance. They push each other and laugh at these strange antics.

'Encore, encore!' they call.

'Don't encourage him,' says his wife.

Down steep steps carved out of the red earth of the mountainside a small boy, no more than three years old, totters towards us pursued by the anxious voice of his mother and an agile elder brother. He slithers to stop a few feet away, hands clasping a dirty rag, almost as large as him, thumb lodged firmly in his mouth. His brown eyes watch us, curious and apprehensive. I would love to photograph these faces but cameras are not welcome.

Yesterday a young goatherd, on the Kik plateau, waved his arms fiercely and shouted loudly when he thought one of our party was about to capture him on film. 'He might lose his soul,' our guide said.

We left Marrakech, a bowl of cacophony, this morning. I've woken in the early hours of each morning to the first call to prayer of the day. The windows of the room at the hotel look out onto a square where most of the buses of the city stop to disgorge their load of workers talking and shouting in loud voices and then pick up a similar number of equally voluble locals. Car horns sound with liberal abandon, just to let everybody know that they are coming in case someone might decide to get in the way.

We've been walking for two hours along this mule track as it winds through the foothills of the mountains and I've forgotten Marrakech. Way behind is Amizmiz, a straggling settlement on the valley floor. Before setting out on our trek, we stopped at its Tuesday market, one of the largest in the Atlas. Squeezing through the solid mass of local traders most in black or grey djellabah, we are tolerated rather than welcomed. Carrots, potatoes, beans, mint, coriander, all straight from the earth and piled high on stalls, cry out to be bought. If only I had somewhere to cook them. But hunger has caught up with me and I start to eat a banana. I look up and see a man pointing at me. Too late, I've forgotten that during Ramadan, Muslims fast between sunrise and sunset. I am offending their religious practices. I stuff the banana into my pocket and forget about it.

Now, from the mosque's minaret, the demanding call to prayer echoes up and across the valley and swirls into my ears. We've left behind the Berber children, the girls showing us their palms stained with henna as they wave goodbye. I can't believe they are to be married just yet.

A kilometre on, it's time to stop for lunch. We are out of sight of the villagers. I find a flat rock to perch on while munching my bread, eggs, cheese, tomatoes and the ever-present orange. Below, the houses of Tizgui stretch down the steep mountainside, piled one on top of the other as though growing from the rusted red rock. Grey smoke spirals through a gaping hole in the roof of one home and drifts across the clear blue sky filling my nostrils with woody incense. Along the sides of the valley, wide terraces have been carved in tiers. From this distance they seem to be gracious landscaped gardens, oases of green set in stony scrub. But these are the fields and orchards where the women toil in their kaleidoscope of coloured dresses. I turn and behind the head of the valley, rolls of orange mounds studded with pine trees give way to beige foothills. Beyond them, sit the High Atlas, easily recognised by a coating of the winter's first snows. Toubkal, the highest peak, is a jagged frosty finger emerging shyly from behind its neighbours. It might have snowed up there but down here the sun is hot. It's 26th December and sunscreen and T-shirts are the order of the day.

The voices around me fade into the distance as I feed on the stillness and singing silence until... the children have found us again. They look longingly at our lunch and I give them what remains of mine. Our guide is not looking.

We have at least another hour's walking before returning along the same route later in the afternoon. I've dropped to the back of the group. This is where the photographers can be found and I have my camera with me. There's a good chance of walking in silence for a while and of having time to spot the most photogenic views. In the middle of the group it's very easy to pace along with my head down, talking and missing the sights. We're joined by a herd of goats. Small and brown, they appear to be shrubs scattered across the hillside until they gather in response to the song of their young herdsman. They cross the track, bleating at us before disappearing into the craggy outcrops. In the distance another group of dwellings straggles our route. I begin to feel a reluctance to walk through another village; it's as though I'm intruding. I wonder how the inhabitants feel about us - we who are materially much more affluent. Maybe I shouldn't be here. But, as I look up, I see the television aerials perched on top of the stone houses. They don't need to see us, to know what they do not have.

But maybe they have something we don't. A simpler life – though one of hard physical work. They are nearer to the earth – directly reliant on nature to provide them with the means to live. That can bring lots of uncertainty. Do they have more faith than most of us in the West? And the women and children I have seen here in the hills laugh a lot even when working. Do they dream of a more fulfilled life? They must have seen through television how women in other cultures live their lives.

A villager invites us into his home for tea. It's mint and very sweet, the national drink in Morocco. We are shown into what seems to be the best room. Rugs are laid on the earth floors and hang on the rough walls. A television lurks in one corner beneath a cloth covering. From time to time children creep around the edge of the door to look at us sipping away. They smile but will come no further. Are they shy or have they been told to keep away? Refreshed, we start on our trek back. The route is busy with farmers returning on their mules from the market, panniers mostly empty.

Dusk falls as our minibus crosses the plain, returning us to Marrakech under a sky washed with rugged crimson and mauve flames. As we near the city, the traffic thickens. Pedestrians, cyclists both pedal and motor, and bus drivers compete for the same space. Those with the loudest horns and greatest nerve triumph. Purple sage night shrouds the lit Booksellers mosque just across the square from our hotel in the Medina. Marrakechis are gathering in souks, cafes and fun fairs to celebrate the end of Ramadan. After dinner, a group of us go into the souk. Progress is slow. I only have to look at some clothes or rugs, and the stall owner starts his sales pitch.

I am back in Marrakech, a furnace of sound.

Spider's Work

come the wane of the ten of moons
weary and lacking of spirit
i loop a hook under the eave
and weave
   and weave
     and weave.

It's a few days since I've returned from Morocco and I know I have been thrown off balance by my experiences there. I don't quite know how it's happened, apart from being aware of discord in our party and feeling sensitive to the noise of Marrakech. But there's been no time to delve any further as I am attending another of the ongoing Voice and Movement courses with Gilles. Ten of us are warming up and it's happened again. My voice is lost in a mêlée of sound. I gasp for breath. *I thought I'd got over this.* But my experiences in Morocco have somehow sensitised me to sound. Back at home I have to plunge into that world of sound I've brought back with me.

One evening, by the light of a candle, I sit at my kitchen table with a pen and a pad of paper. I allow my hand to draw from my world the sounds that have troubled me, and place them around the periphery of a spider's web laid on the page. Here are the culprits, the voices, the figures. They instruct 'write this, not that'; demand 'minister to me'; beseech 'come my way, I need you'; complain 'your voice is flat, sharp, not deep enough'; manipulate 'do what I want, never mind what you want'; command 'leave the writing'. They are threatening, severing, whining, shouting, browbeating, sneering, nagging, harassing, clamouring, imperious, exacting and deafening. The spider emerges. She wraps each of these words of cloudy quartz in her silken thread and with one final swift movement draws them to the centre of her web.

My being is suffocated.

♫

This suffocation means it's time to explore death. What does it mean for me?

Over a period of months I sit, from time to time at home, in meditation. My task is to make affirmations. 'Death is inevitable.' 'The timing of my death is indefinite.' 'What will make my life more meaningful?' 'What will make my death more meaningful?' I must name the emotions these words arouse in me and explore the feelings, the sensations in my body. The emotions are just the names attached to what is the basic energy of my life. This is not a task for my mind to undertake. It is for my body to experience. Recollections, remembrances appear in between the meditations. There is a timelessness about these months.

And so I sit and chant.

'The timing of my death is indefinite.' 'Death is inevitable.'

Here is desolation.

My body is cold through to its core. My hands are ice-bound. A pain aches in my absent breast. Death. No. An ending.

Here is sorrow.

I see myself in the hospital bed after my mastectomy. I cannot, must not sleep. I am on guard. Clutching my body. Frozen. No one here. No one holding me. A virus of worry running through my body. Death. No. An ending.

Here is tiredness.

No. Monumental weariness wastes my limbs. I am carrying my mother as she lies in a hospital bed. My strength seeps out of me. The cripple falls to the floor. Death. No. An ending.

Here is rejection.

My body shrivels. Blackness. Death. No. An ending.

Here is despair.

My voice is not heard. Death. No. An ending.

Here is warmth.

It congregates in my heart. Tremors creep through my body.

My silent mantra repeats over and over again.

Here is irritation.

Hold it. It expands.

Here is isolation. Death. No. An ending.

Linger with it.

Here are thorns in my flesh.

I am spurned. Remembrances of never being able to sing, "He Was Despised" from *Messiah*, without crying. Death. No. An ending.

My voice is buried in the earth. Death. No. An ending.

I dig and dig. I cannot reach its heart

I rage and rage.

I cannot reach it.

Seize the rage.

Harness it.

It lashes out. Do not come near me.

The Viper. It protects from invasion. Venom streams.

Hold it.

I dream

I am leaving the home my mother made for me. Wandering along a road. She will be angry if I do not return. A man walks from behind me. I do not know him. He puts his arm around my shoulders. He walks on and looks back at me smiling in support.

Snake, which whispered its shape to me, which Earthworm had shifted into, has returned but this time it is Viper. I take out my pastel colours and draw it. It is unlocking itself within the labyrinth but it is twisted round its heart. It has a jewel in its mouth which it must protect until it is safe to reveal it. I am the lover and the loved. Coaxing. Sounding the viper's hiss. I have a thread.

Where will it lead me?

Who Sings?

After tilling soil
with her hoe she releases
engaging her soul.

Drawn by Ariadne's thread, I fly from day into a night filled with pale moon, flaring planets and winking stars until the sun appears hovering on the horizon. Below, the ground begins to unfold the Songlines made by humans across the land since the beginning of time. To those who can hear them, they tell of all that is known.

Buried in my addled head, I stumble along a path. I left home on Thursday. Cardiff to Amsterdam, where I was nearly bumped off the next flight to Minneapolis – 98 degrees: then to Denver – mile high city. Three planes, three time changes and it's still Thursday. Here at the Sunrise Ranch in the foothills of the Rocky Mountains in Colorado is where I must find the answer to my question.

Who Sings?

'Hi. I'm Nell.' Her grey hair is knotted to lie on the nape of her neck. With pale skin and blue eyes she looks the epitome of a genteel English woman but with a southern drawl.

'Saw you walking around and thought I'd introduce myself. I live here.'

All I know about the ranch is that it's home to a community of over a hundred people calling themselves the Emissaries of Light.

'I'm Elizabeth. I'm here for the Healing Sounds Course with Jonathan Goldman.'

'Great. All that singing and chanting is good for us residents. Where you from?'

'Wales.'

'I've been there, to Machynlleth. Do you know the Williams, Sian and John?'

'No, I don't. I'm from Cardiff, in the south.'

Mixed with a delicate mauve and pink sunset and a full moon rising in a purple sky is a sweaty aroma loaded on the heavy air.

'Nell, what's that smell?'

'That's a skunk. It's expired somewhere we can't find it. Charlie's onto it.'

The acid stink has got up my nose and comes with me to my room where I fall into bed.

Who Sings?

I surface from my bed the following morning. Charlie hasn't found the skunk yet. The sun, out of an empty sky, is baking the rusty Rockies. I've arrived a couple of days before the course is due to begin. As I make my way towards a lone pine tree up the hill behind the ranch, Nell appears from nowhere.

'Going rambling?'

'I thought I'd explore a bit.'

'Just watch out for bears and snakes, honey. Don't run.'

When I reach the shelter of the pine, I sit on a stone placed as though it's been waiting for me. I jump up. Snakes. But all's clear. I go through the visualisation I've brought with me. I see my soul descending through my body, cleaning all my windows so that whatever needs to shine through can do so.

Who sings?

A breeze hums through the needles and a humming bird swoops in, hovers for a minute and moves on. I follow it.

Three hours later, I am returning with my empty water bottle and a piece of red rock. I lost the humming bird pretty soon after setting out and there've been no bears or snakes. I can't remember what I have seen except a place where there's nowhere to hide.

As I pass my pine, a streak of lightning thrusts out of a lurking black cloud, which lets go of its load. Just three minutes worth. I watch steam rising off my jeans.

Back on the ranch Nell is waiting.

She starts speaking as though we've been having a long conversation. 'I came here after my husband died. For a few weeks, to reflect. Where was I going with my life?'

'And you stayed?'

'Not right away. But I knew this was the place for me.'

'I envy you. I wish I had that kind of certainty.'

'You need to listen to where you are meant to be.' She enunciates "listen" clearly.

'Thanks Nell.'

Arriving early for the course has given me too much time in which to conjure up demons about this, my latest expedition. That night I slide into bed and…

I dream

I am with my mother. She is meant to be giving a talk about nursing. She has sheaves of papers and wants me to find the right place for her to start. I can't make sense of her mound of notes. There are too many. Perhaps they are not the right ones? Shall I throw them away?

In the morning, this dream seems to echo the confusion about why I am here. No it's not that. I do know why I'm here. What I don't know is why I feel so afraid of being here. I think "Claudia", the fearful one and Golden Girl are in battle mode.

At breakfast, most of the other course participants have arrived. I sit next to two of them who know each other. They banter away. *They are so much more knowledgeable, attractive, clever, funny than I am.* Others are talking with brightness about wanting the light of love. *Do they know the darkness? Or are they pretending it's not there?*

The sessions are not starting until this afternoon so I go and do my laundry but as soon as I am back in my room I am in "Claudia's" clutches, gulping with fear.

I want to go home. Back to my friends, my house. That's where my heart is.

Oh no "Claudia" that is not so. It's ok.

Who Sings?

I take myself off to my pine tree and listen to the hot wind singing through the needles. I think about the woman who stopped me as I walked back from the laundry block. 'Hi there. I've seen you walking around and thought I should introduce myself. I'm Mary. My family lives here.'

'Hello. I'm Elizabeth. I'm here for the sound healing course.'

'Jonathan's level two course. Lucky you. He's just had the level one. I quite envy you all that sound and chanting. Nice talking to you. See you around.'

I wonder who she has seen walking around. A sad, lonely person, full of apprehension and homesickness. Trying to hide from herself. Or maybe she's seen a me who Nell has described as dignified and gracious. Or has she seen the eager me who is anticipating great things. *Come out wherever you are Golden Girl.*

It's time to remind myself of the myth of Ariadne, the ancient Goddess of Crete. According to her story, she paid out, to her hero, her clue of thread so that he could find his way to the centre of the great labyrinth of Knossos. There he killed the Minotaur and using the thread, found his way out again. The myth symbolises the struggle of humanity to challenge its instinctual and unconscious behaviours and reach conscious illumination.

Who Sings?

The first session is underway. We are twenty-eight participants, together with teachers, sitting around the edge of the Green Ridge Octagonal Room of the Conference Centre at the ranch. As well as from many of the states in the USA including New York, California, Illinois, Massachusetts, Texas, Nevada, Florida, we come from Canada, Argentina, Italy, Chile, New Mexico and Wales. Outside the window is an ornamental pond filled with lilies. And the sun is intense. We introduce ourselves. My name is Elizabeth. My colour is Gold. My intention is to know...

Who Sings?

That evening we chart the maze with chanting...

OM NAMAH SHIVAYA
I pay homage to the energy of the Lord Shiva
OM NAMAH SHIVAYA
I pay homage to the energy of the Lord Shiva
OM NAMAH SHIVAYA
I pay homage to the energy of the Lord Shiva...

A chant to Shiva who transforms negative energy.

I remember once, when trying to find the note 'Ma', that Gilles said if I placed my breath through the point in the middle of the sternum called the Shiva point my 'Ma' would be transformed. It would be freed of any negative energy associated with mother. And it was.

OM NAMAH SHIVAYA
I pay homage to the energy of the Lord Shiva
OM NAMAH SHIVAYA
I pay homage to the energy of the Lord Shiva
OM NAMAH SHIVAYA
I pay homage to the energy of the Lord Shiva...

I sink to sit on the floor, gazing at a mass of lit candles on the altar. I hear the voices rise from a fiery well, travelling across the desert, down the ages. I rise...

OM NAMAH SHIVAYA
I pay homage to the energy of the Lord Shiva
OM NAMAH SHIVAYA
I pay homage to the energy of the Lord Shiva
OM NAMAH SHIVAYA
I pay homage to the energy of the Lord Shiva...

An hour later, I walk out into a night of full moon and fall into bed.

♫

As on the level one course with Jonathan, which I attended five years ago, harmonics play an important part of the work. We tone using the vowel sounds 'Uh', 'Ooo', 'Oh', 'Ah', 'Eye', 'Ay', 'Eee' as mantras on one breath up each of the seven chakras.

We do it out loud, then silently, and finally whispering. I feel the tingling energy moving through my body and then sadness. I have to wait to know what this is about.

We spend a day toning from the silence of no talking. We start at nine in the morning and finish twelve hours later. Laid out on the centre of the floor of the Green Ridge room is a tre-vesica, three overlapping circles. This is one of the forms of sacred geometry. Such forms carry archetypal memories, the two main ones being the feminine and the masculine. The tre-vesica relates to detachment from ourselves and others; witnessing our relationships from a place of non-judgement. *Oh yes, let go of control, of ideas of what is perfect.*

We split into groups and each group takes it in turns to sit in the labyrinth of the circles and tone for one and a half hours at intervals throughout the day. In between, sometimes I walk outside, and hear the electricity wires and pylons humming, even the buildings hum. At other times I sit or stand in some of the geometric shapes, which hang around the room, listening to the toning. In a corner of the room, one participant ceremoniously prepares Japanese tea. I witness, as though from afar, people taking their cups and sipping as he mimes instructions for the observation of the ritual. And I partake as well. At suppertime, we eat in silence. I taste, as though for the first time, the chicken, the beans, the potatoes. As the day draws to a close, we all gather to tone together for the last hour before threading our way through the labyrinth.

♫

Saruah Sarah Benson, who has joined Jonathan as one of the facilitators, takes us on singing and sound journeys. I, like everyone else, am lying on the floor. Sun is streaming through the windows. I draw breath up as a sigh from Mother Earth and breathe it out to Grandfather Sky, repeating it up and down the scale several times, imagining the marriage of Earth and Sky. Placing my hands on any part of my body that I sense needs healing, I imagine myself in the waters of Mother Earth. I make the sounds of the ocean rippling, washing, tumbling, surging around and over me. Images of otters, dolphins and fish emerge and I play in sound with them. Gradually I sink back into silence as the sounds of the sea fade. I am back on the earth.

Saruah asks us to sing to a partner. That's all.

My partner is Nora. 'I'm from Nebraska. I'm a healer in my local Church,' she tells me.

Nora is a precise woman. I've heard her questions and contributions. Challenging anything that does not fit with her beliefs. I look at her. Dressed in a pleated skirt and trim blouse, with white skin and crisp silver hair, she encompasses, what seems to me, absolute certainty in her way.

What on earth do I sing to her? Do I have any connection with her?
I look into her sparky blue eyes and she holds my gaze.
Ariadne, help me.

I wait until…

My lungs expand with breath, which sneaks to fill my heart. Into my imagination swells a large ebony woman with a chocolate voice. A lullaby, unknown to me, emerges for Nora. When it is spent, it fades into the place it came from.

Tears slip from Nora's eyes and her face softens.

I am filled with uncomprehending wonder.

Who Sings?

♫

One evening, in groups of seven, we blow the Peruvian whistling vessels. As I listen to the other groups, I start yawning hugely – a signal that my energy is moving, changing. When I start blowing, I feel the sound strongly in my right ear. From there it moves down the same side of my body as though sneaking through nooks and crannies, clearing them out. I hear the vessels create a low moaning sound, which is joined gradually by the tinkling of bells in a gentle breeze. How does this happen? Everybody seems to have different accounts of what they have heard, how they are affected when we exchange experiences afterwards. I notice that the low level headache which I have had since I arrived in Colorado has disappeared. I go out into the moonlit night and open my arms out like wings.

If I could fly, I would.

♫

Tara appears again as, another evening, thunder rumbles over the mountains. We chant and dance the maze with her.

OM TARE TU TARE TURE SVAHA
Homage to you, Divine Tara, Radiant Mother of Compassion
OM TARE TU TARE TURE SVAHA
Homage to you, Divine Tara, Radiant Mother of Compassion
OM TARE TU TARE TURE SVAHA
Homage to you, Divine Tara, Radiant Mother of Compassion

White Tara, the Goddess of Peace and Compassion. *I do have a job to let myself hear and act on her message.*

OM TARE TU TARE TURE SVAHA
Homage to you, Divine Tara, Radiant Mother of Compassion
OM TARE TU TARE TURE SVAHA
Homage to you, Divine Tara, Radiant Mother of Compassion
OM TARE TU TARE TURE SVAHA
Homage to you, Divine Tara, Radiant Mother of Compassion

Green Tara, the dynamic Goddess overcoming obstacles, saviour from physical and spiritual danger. *Yes, I need to know and own these aspects of Tara.*

I dance my way, under an orange moon, to bed. The rumbling thunder has disappeared.

♫

The course is nearing its end. A bright morning outside finds us in the Green Ridge room, walking around in a circle, humming with lips closed and jaw open, while Saruah drums. I practice opening and closing my jaws so that the sound, which comes out, is relaxed and tuneful. I stop by a course member and we look into each other's eyes and I say, 'Hello again. It's been a long time.' I carry on walking and someone stops me. He says, 'Hello again. It's been a long time.' We move on, greeting each other in this way several times. I am left realising that it is rare to look into the eyes of a person whom I barely know but recognise an ancient connection between us. Despite our differences we are of oneness.

Saruah asks us to return to our seats. 'It's time to sing the song of your soul, if you choose. The rest of us will hum quietly as you do so.'

The invitation hangs in the air.

A woman moves to sit in the centre of our circle. A melody full of Jewish yearning creeps around the room. She finishes.

I sit waiting.

Nora moves to stand next to Saruah. Her bell-like voice echoes around the rafters. She finishes.

I sit waiting.

A hand in the middle of my back urges me forward. I look behind me. There is no one there. I move to the centre of the circle.

What on earth am I doing here? Ariadne, what am I meant to sing?
I'll pay out my thread. Search the maze. I'll be here.

A hushed sound forms in the deeps of the ravine. I nurture it. Inspire it.

It snakes through grottoes, boring into bone, seeping into blood, rising on the wind, suckling organs, firing cells.

I hone it.

It warms me.

It emerges propelled forward, leaning backward, swaying sideways, lifting up, pressing down, melting into its core.

A golden serpent uncoiling as it traces the maze of Songlines.

I finish and Saruah announces, 'That is all the time we have.'

I blink. I am still sitting in my sound. A moment's delay, and I would have missed this opportunity.

I have come home to the Song of My Soul.

Some Books that have helped me on my journey;

Angelo, Jack, *Your Healing Power: a comprehensive guide to channelling your healing energy,* London, Piatkus Books, 1994/2007

Angelo, Jack and Angelo, Jan, *Sacred Healing: a soul-based approach to subtle energy medicine,* London, Piatkus Books, 2001

Angelo, Jack, *The Distant Healing Handbook: how to send healing to people, animals, the environment and global trouble spots,* London, Piatkus Books, 2007

Armstrong, Karen, *The Spiral Staircase: A Memoir,* London, Harper Perennial, 2005

Arrien, Angeles, *The Four-Fold Way: Walking the Paths of the Warrior, Teacher, Healer and Visionary,* New York, HarperSanFrancisco, 1993

Axline, Virginia M, *Dibs in Search of Self: The Moving Story of an Emotionally Lost Child Who Found his Own Way Back,* London, Penguin Books, 1990

Baring, Anne and Cashford, Jules, *The Myth Of The Goddess: Evolution of an Image,* London, Penguin Books, 1993

De Villiers, Marq and Hirtle, Sheila, *Into Africa,* London, Phoenix, 1998

Estés, Clarissa Pinkola, *Women Who Run With The Wolves: Contacting the Power of the Wild Woman,* London, Rider, 1992

Field, Joanna, (Milner, Marion), *A Life of One's Own,* London, Virago Press, 1986

Field, Joanna, (Milner, Marion), *An Experiment In Leisure,* London, Virago Press, 1986

Fuller, Alexandra, *Don't Let's Go To The Dogs Tonight: An African Childhood,* London, Picador, 2002

Gibran, Kahlil, *The Prophet*, London, Penguin Classics, 2002

Godwin, Peter, *Mukiwa: A White Boy in Africa*, London, Picador, 1997

Goldberg, Natalie, *Writing Down the Bones: Freeing the Writer Within*, Boston, Shambala Publications, 1986

Goldman, Jonathan, *Healing Sounds: The Power of Harmonics*, London, Element Books, 1992

Herbert, Marie, *Healing Quest: A Journey of Transformation*, London, Rider, 1996

Hillman, James, *The Soul's Code: In Search of Character and Calling*, London, Bantam Books, 1997

Kidd, Sue Monk, *The Dance Of The Dissident Daughter: A woman's Journey from Christian Tradition to the Sacred Feminine*, New York, HarperCollins, 1996

Lalla, translated by Barks, Coleman, *Naked Song*, Athens, GA, Maypop Books, 1992

Moore, Thomas, *Care Of The Soul: How to Add Depth and Meaning to Your Everyday Life*, London, Piatkus, 1992

Moore, Thomas, *The Re-Enchantment of Everyday Life*, London, Hodder and Stoughton, 1997

Sams, Jamie, *The 13 Original Clan Mothers: Your Sacred Path to Discovering the Gifts, Talents & Abilities of the Feminine Through the Ancient Teachings of the Sisterhood*, New York, HarperCollins, 1994

Starbird, Margaret, *The Woman With The Alabaster Jar: Mary Magdalen and the Holy Grail*, Santa Fe, New Mexico, Bear & Co, 1993

Valentis, Mary, and Devane, Anne, *Female Rage: Unlocking Its Secrets, Claiming Its Power*, New York, Carol Southern Books, 1994

About the Author

Eleven years ago, Elizabeth Jones gave up a successful career in the Civil Service to become a counsellor, a writer, and to sing and travel. She combines her counselling skills and the experience of finding her own voice, in working with individuals and groups who seek the voice inside them. She lives in Cardiff.

About the Artist

Kay Leverton lives in Tredegar, South Wales where she seeks answers to the big questions such as 'who am I?' through her art and poetry. To find out more about Kay and her work visit her web site at www.artfromthesoul.co.uk

ORDER FORM

You can order further copies of this book direct from
Spiderloom Books

FREE UK DELIVERY

To order further copies of *Soul Song*
please send the coupon below to:

Spiderloom Books
11 Meadow Street
Cardiff CF11 9PY

Alternatively, you may order via our web site:

www.soul-song.co.uk

Please allow 28 days for delivery. Do not send cash. Offer subject to availability. We do not share or sell our customers' details.

Please send me ___ copies of *Soul Song*.

I enclose a UK bank cheque or postal order, payable to Spiderloom Books for £___, @ £9.99 per copy

Name: _____

Address: _____

_____

_____

email: _____

Please tick box if you do not wish to receive ☐
further information from Spiderloom Books.

Spiderloom
Books